D0623896

NURSERY DESIGN

NURSERY DESIGN

CREATING A PERFECT ENVIRONMENT FOR YOUR CHILD

TEXT BY BARBARA ARIA

PHOTOGRAPHS BY ANDREW BORDWIN

ADDITIONAL PHOTOGRAPHS BY STEVE MOORE AND TONY GIAMMARINO

BANTAM BOOKS

NEW YORK • TORONTO • LONDON • SYDNEY • AUCKLAND

NURSERY DESIGN
A Bantam Book/April 1990

NURSERY DESIGN was produced by Running Heads Incorporated
55 West 21st Street
New York, New York 10010

Editor: Sarah Kirshner
Designer: Liz Trovato
Production Manager: Linda Winters
Managing Editor: Lindsey Crittenden

Typeset by Trufont Typographers
Color Separations by Hong Kong Scanner Craft Co., Ltd.

MR. RABBIT AND THE LOVELY PRESENT by Charlotte Zolotow
Text copyright © 1962 by Charlotte Zolotow
Reprinted by permission of Harper & Row, Publishers, Inc.,
and The Bodley Head

All rights reserved.
Copyright © 1990 by Running Heads Incorporated.
No part of this book may be reproduced or transmitted in any form or by any
means, electronic or mechanical, including photocopying, recording, or by any
information storage and retrieval system, without permission in writing from
the publisher. For information address: Bantam Books.

Library of Congress Cataloging-in-Publication Data

Aria, Barbara.
Nursery Design : creating a perfect environment for your
child / text by Barbara Aria ; photography by Andrew Bordwin ;
design by Liz Trovato.
p.   cm.
Includes bibliographical references.
ISBN 0-553-05758-8
1. Interior decoration.   2. Nurseries.   I. Title.
NK2117.N87A75   1990
747.7′7 — dc20   89-17543
                                                          CIP

Published simultaneously in the United States and Canada

Bantam Books are published by Bantam Books, a division of Bantam Doubleday
Dell Publishing Group, Inc. Its trademark, consisting of the words "Bantam
Books" and the portrayal of a rooster, is Registered in U.S. Patent and Trademark
Office and in other countries. Marca Registrada. Bantam Books, 666 Fifth
Avenue, New York, New York 10103.

Printed and bound in Singapore by Times Offset Pte Ltd.

0 9 8 7 6 5 4 3 2 1

ACKNOWLEDGMENTS

This book would not have been possible without the contributions of the architects, designers, decorative painters, and craftspeople who shared with us their work, and their unique understanding of children's environments. Thanks to Laura Dabrowski of Laura D.'s Folk-Art Furniture, Mindy Isaacoff of Lewis of London, James Allen Smith, and Viola Icken and the Mansions and Millionaires Designers Showcase '89. I am indebted to all those who helped, and also to the parents and children who allowed us into their homes and let us photograph their nurseries. And many thanks to Andrew Bordwin, who so enthusiastically met the challenge of photographing those nurseries and children's rooms.

My gratitude also to Marta Hallett and Ellen Milionis of Running Heads Incorporated, who supported my efforts, and to the staff of Running Heads, especially Sarah Kirshner, who gave me much encouragement and editorial guidance, Ellie Watson, who researched and organized the location photography against all odds, Lindsey Crittenden, and Linda Winters. Thanks are also due to Coleen O'Shea of Bantam Books for her support.

There are many others to whom I am grateful for help and advice, but most of all I want to thank my daughter Zoe, who let me ransack her bookshelves in my search for the inspiration to be found in children's literature.

CONTENTS

▲ *Simple furnishings and neutral surface colors, above, are brightened by a circus poster and hand-painted floor figures.*

INTRODUCTION

Design in the nursery has always tended to reflect our feelings about childhood. Today we generally understand those first years of life as a short span of almost magical innocence, or wonderment. We know it as a time of intense thirst for experience, both physical and intellectual, coupled with a real need for enveloping security and warmth. It is also a time in which the child's sense of individuality and confidence are formed.

And so design in the nursery today is more than a matter of aesthetics or practicalities. Design in the nursery addresses the issue of psychological and physical space — what kind of space feels good to a tiny infant, or to a child as it learns to crawl, walk, and jump; the issue of personal identity and gender identity, and how these can be fostered when the nursery must be shared by more than one child; the issue of growth, both physical and mental — which colors or patterns does a newborn infant find most stimulating and enjoyable, and how can design elements be adapted as the child develops more complex needs, such as the need for fantasy.

As a place intended and designed for the special needs of babyhood and early childhood, the nursery's revival follows a long period during which it was pronounced all but dead. During much of this century the nursery was the most forgotten of domestic spaces. It was a repository for outmoded and worn furnishings handed down from the living room or master bedroom, an environment distinguished by stick-on nursery decals and perhaps a baby pink or baby blue wall, and, with the post-war thrust for modernity, a place devoted to adult-centered issues of hygiene and practicality, rarely to aesthetic or psychological experiences. "Actually, frills in a nursery are impractical. . . . They are hard to keep clean, they get in the way and after a few weeks in the company of a lusty child they will probably be in shreds," went a typical piece of advice from the *Woman's Home Companion Household Book* of 1948.

There was, it seemed, very little room in modern life for nostalgia or romance. Besides, hardly anybody had baby nurses anymore (and it is from the baby nurse that the nursery derives its name); few could afford the space to set aside two rooms for a child, as in the Victorian day and night nurseries; and as the present-day family evolved, the whole concept of babies leading separate lives in separate rooms came to seem like an anomaly. The living room and kitchen quickly became the rooms that were the centers of baby life, in which the whole family, including its youngest members, could gather.

Even in more recent years architectural and home design magazines, while devoting pages of pictures and words to the most stylish of projects, have seldom offered even the slightest glimpse of a nursery. The most painstakingly compiled reference works and indexes in the field of architecture and design give extensive listings for living rooms, kitchens, bathrooms, garages, hunting lodges, and the maintenance and repair of royal palaces. Yet they contain no distinct references for the rooms in which babies and children are nurtured — the rooms, in fact, in which some of our future designers are at this very moment lying in cribs or creeping across floors, exploring their surroundings while absorbing colors and patterns.

Nursery design was once a legitimate concern even among the most prominent architects and designers. An entire exhibition devoted to Art Nouveau–related nursery design at the Musée Galliera in Paris in 1912 is just one example. Today, design professionals and parents alike are rediscovering the delights of creating special worlds for children, for these small worlds can accommodate the longed-for flights of fancy or touches of humor that might be considered risky in any other room.

The nursery is no longer the haunt of nurse and her charge. Ideally it is a room shared by parents and children, for one or twelve hours a day. It is a gift to the child of all that the parent holds most dear, a sharing of childhood memories and a passing on of pleasurable aesthetic experiences in a form that a child can understand and enjoy.

As such the nursery weaves together grown-up style and aesthetics with an understanding of a child's sensibility. After half a century of modernism we have come to associate sophisticated design with an intensely restrained style.

▲ *A common theme of bunnies from children's classics such as* The Velveteen Rabbit *and* Peter Rabbit *unifies the nursery, above, with its hand-painted wall panels based on illustrations from Beatrix Potter.*

But the cool, modern solutions that were once considered the height of sophisticated interior design have, in the past decade, given way to a new form of design sophistication that is on the whole perfectly suited to the nursery—and nowhere is this more evident than in the return of decoration and color to surfaces that were for so long blank.

The challenge presented by the nursery is often one of turning a bland, shapeless environment into a small world that nurtures, stimulates, and pleases from day one through all the changes of babyhood and early childhood. From the hand-looming of individualized rugs to the painting of trompe l'oeil murals or stenciled friezes, the nursery is benefiting from the return of artisanship and craftsmanship to home design.

Environmental psychology has played a large role in shaping the nursery of today. Having recognized that infants often need a gradual transition from the close uterine environment, we are bringing cradles and bassinets out of historical storage back into the nursery. Knowing that small children feel more independent and in control when their environment is scaled to their size, we are reviving the tradition of scaled-down nursery furnishings and lowering such space-defining architectural details as chair or picture rails. Great strides have been made toward understanding the bond between newborn babies and their parents. We know how crucial that bond is, yet we also accept that parental love does not always come immediately or automatically, and that style and atmosphere in the nursery—whether it comes from a nostalgically flounced bassinet or from a huge, glowing crayon night-light—can encourage those loving feelings when the baby is screaming and it's two o'clock in the morning.

New technologies and materials have also played a role. Where practical concerns such as safety and hygiene previously served to limit nursery design options, today's easy-care fabrics, growable and multipurpose furnishings, high tech fixtures, and laminates make it possible to create the most fanciful of nursery styles without sacrificing function or breaking budgets. Because, though a sterile, overly protective environment has no appeal for babies or children, an environment full of small dangers in which the child has to be constantly watched by a hovering adult can be even less appealing. As the writer Herman Muthesius said in his now-classic work *The English House* (1904): "The nursery is a place where the children can enjoy a full measure of peace without their lives being disturbed by the activities of the grown-ups."

The nursery represents the world of the child as it is seen through the eyes of the adults who are closest and dearest. When that world is sensitively portrayed, it gives the child images to treasure, comfort to ease the day's hurts, a friendly warmth to reassure him that all is safe even after the lights are dimmed, and every possible opportunity for his imagination to turn day-to-day nursery life into a fantastic adventure.

▲ *Holding a cuddly trio of stuffed nursery animals, a woven basket painted white and adorned with pink ribbon and eyelet ruffle, above, doubles as an attractive display and a cozy home for nighttime crib friends.*

BUILDING BLOCKS:

1

INTERIOR DESIGN STYLES IN THE NURSERY

▲ *Floral wallpaper, wicker headboard, antique pillows, and framed prints create a Victorian feeling, above.*

Once upon a time, not so long ago, *style* was a very grown-up word, like *gourmet* or *tuxedo*. Back then, interior style meant a choice between traditional or modern, and in the world of "good design" traditional choices were seen as something of a sin. The ideal home was an attractive, efficient shelter. Progress was the buzzword; the past belonged in museums. While the first astronauts orbited space and the first computers whirred in their specially controlled environments, designers used glass, chrome, and the new miracle plastics as expressions of the new age, and created interiors that were in different ways reflections of Le Corbusier's modernist edict that the house be "a machine for living."

"Never hang draperies in an infant's room," "Linoleum is the most successful floor covering," advised the *Woman's Home Companion Household Book* as early as 1948. While adults discussed labor-saving kitchen schemes that would give them more time with the baby, the baby played in a nursery that was clean, safe, practical, and almost completely devoid of charm or comfort.

The nursery as many of today's parents knew it as children was a space segregated stylistically from the rest of the home. Designer nurseries and furnishings in up-to-the-minute styles were scarce, and those that did exist—such as a complete nursery set of skeletal, tubular metal furnishings designed in the thirties by K. E. Orta, a clear Plexiglas crib of the early seventies, or a 1961 bassinet made of cane on a tubular metal stand, lined and hooded in pale blue and yellow nylon—tended to have very little to do with the needs and likes of little children. Besides, most of these cutting-edge designs were imported from Europe and attracted only ultrasophisticated parents. Whatever the style of the rest of the home, most contemporary nurseries featured easy-care plastics in common-sense hospital colors, with bunny decals or gaily colored fabrics and bright mobiles representing the prime concessions to childhood.

In recent years babies have been known to attend dinner parties dressed in tuxedo playsuits, and the vocabulary relating to early childhood has expanded to include words like *gourmet* and *style*. Adults, meanwhile, having turned their attention from the efficiency of style to style as physical and emotional comfort, are coming up with environments that are often inspired by regional and historical designs. Many of these updated or reinterpreted design styles translate easily to the nursery.

The creation of specific design styles in the nursery, as in the rest of the home, has gone hand in hand with a revival of craftsmanship on all levels, making it possible to borrow a seventeenth-century stencil pattern for an Early American–style nursery ceiling, or to update a frieze from a Victorian nursery. The process has also been fueled and influenced by new technologies and materials that make it possible to install a lightweight Doric column or to reproduce pieces of classical trim, complete with angelic *putti* heads, on self-adhesive wallpaper panels.

It is often possible to create an authentic copy of a period nursery, using antique or reproduction furnishings. But historical and regional design styles tend to be freely reinterpreted in the nursery for the sake of practicality, safety, comfort, and ease. Whether the nursery is Victorian, Mediterranean, Shaker, or modern in spirit, it becomes so through the use of particular colors, decorative details, shapes, materials, and motifs that are inherent to the chosen style.

Given a free interpretation, almost any style can now be adapted to the nursery, so the world of the child can be designed to flow from the rest of the house, or to be a room like no other. Parents, who will probably end up spending a fair amount of time in the nursery, can create an environment that accommodates their own feelings about design and style. Those who dream of cuddling the baby amidst a confection of frothy lace and ribbon can do so; those who shrink at the sight of frills and flowers can have a classic, Bauhaus nursery in red, yellow, and blue.

Style decisions are usually based on a combination of interrelated factors. One's sense of aesthetics, or what looks good to the individual eye, is often a gut response, a physiological reaction. Quite often a design style is chosen to preserve the architectural integrity of a period home. In

▲ *Handmade quilts and simple dolls piled into rag baskets, above, help to give the nursery a country flavor.*

▲ *Traditionally designed nurseries, like fairy tales, teddy bears, and toy trains, have a timeless, classic feeling, above.*

other cases certain colors, textures, and forms inherent in a particular style may carry pleasant, personal associations to parents decorating a nursery, bringing to mind a childhood home, or a memorable vacation.

Most forms of traditional or country styling convey a sense of continuity and family values that make a home, and especially a new home in an unfamiliar neighborhood, seem more secure. Perhaps it is for this reason that the heirloom look, suggestive of the ties that bind generations, is enjoying such popularity today, just as it did in the fast-changing Victorian era. In the nursery, traditional styles evoke childhoods past, and stress the unchanging and universal nature of birth and nurturance.

Babies and small children have limited powers of association. But we now know that a strong sense of aesthetics exists from the youngest age. A baby's response to style is purely sensory — taste without the influence of fashion or association. Babies are developmentally inclined to like the look (and sometimes the taste) of clear colors, contrasts, strong patterns, tactile textures. As they grow into toddlers and children, they develop a taste for fantasy that is often based on the storybooks they request nightly.

The child's response to architectural design is intuitive, improvisational. A Doric or Ionic column, for instance, means adventure; it may be the perfect thing to run around, to ambush from, or for a game of peekaboo. Children also like to mimic the adult world as they see it in their own homes. Often the most successful nurseries are those that integrate a child's sensibility within a design scheme that reflects the style of the adult areas of the home. It is not surprising, then, that certain design styles have come to dominate design in today's nursery. Whether historical, regional, or contemporary, these are styles that reflect at one and the same time current fashions in home design and the tastes of babies and small children.

EARLY AMERICAN

The folk style developed by the people of eighteenth-century America has in recent years become one of the most popular in nursery design. Its naive charm, its simple, sturdy furniture, and its rhythmic decorative qualities make it particularly appropriate for babies, while the clear, often childlike stencil designs characteristic of Early American interiors have been recognized as an ingenious way of bringing vivid color and images into small, dark rooms. Early American is a homespun style of practically bare essentials made attractive through down-to-earth decorative details. Its classic lines, its serenity and honesty make it a timeless style, at home in houses both traditional and modern, and in rooms for boys and girls of all ages.

Early American style reflects the realities faced by the people of eighteenth-century America, as well as their boldest aspirations. The austerity of log cabin living had given way to the relative ease of life in clapboard "saltboxes," many of which had grown with the family, room by room, from one-room frame houses. For the first time in many homes there was a room for the children, often under the eaves. And with the very beginnings of a new view of children as blossoming individuals, rather than as slightly unruly miniature adults, came the introduction of a few simple wooden toys and children's books — rocking horses "to teach children to ride," as the advertisements claimed; chapbooks and toy books filled with moral tales and illustrated with bold, black and white woodcuts; and Mother Goose books, "calculated to amuse children and excite them to sleep," as an early, 1791 edition claims.

Having won the battle for survival, Americans now yearned for a measure of refined domesticity in their lives and homes; news of fashionable life was reaching even small villages from the towns and cities of the new nation, and many settlers remembered the rich decorative traditions of their ancestral Europe. But times were still hard. Like the interiors of many contemporary urban homes, rooms were tiny and basic, with low ceilings and small

▲ *An Early American–style "saltbox" dollhouse, with porch and steeply pitched roof, sets the scene in this delightful nursery tableau, above. The unusual wallpaper, patterned all over with Asian-inspired motifs, recalls the naive imagery of Early American stencil designs.*

▶ *A delicately woven wreath is suggestive of times gone by, while a small collection of new and antique hand-crafted wooden toys creates an Early American flavor in this nursery, right. The simplicity of the ceramic-based lamp and butter-yellow paper enhance the homely quality of the styling.*

windows. Few families could yet afford much in the way of home embellishment, and many materials were still scarce; wallpaper, for instance, was available and even advertised in newspapers, but because of a scarcity of local rags, paper wall coverings had to be imported from Europe, making them too expensive for most people.

Rather than an authentic copy, today's Early American–style nursery is a tribute to the inventiveness, skill, and thrift with which the average American transformed the home with the plainest of materials, creating a cheery center for family life. Since glass was expensive, windows were small and many-paned, sparingly yet prettily dressed with a short, single panel of lightly shirred calico hung by tabs from a wooden pole. Native woods—dark cherry, warm pine, creamy colored maple, and hickory—were handcrafted into basic, solidly constructed furnishings with simply turned legs or posts. The same woods, often painted in muted blues or greens, were used for simple architectural detailing such as wainscoting and chair rails, which gave a sense of dignity to otherwise meager rooms.

The artful use of recycled fabrics to make quilts and rugs provided the early American home with simple comfort and decorative qualities that remain central to the style today. Patchwork quilts, filled with soft feathers, were made from a very limited range of fabrics and featured simple emblematic motifs—the red barn, the star, the log cabin—and brightened dark bedrooms and sleeping lofts. Rag rugs, woven from scraps of outgrown clothing, added interesting textures and colors to dark board floors. Pillows, covered in calico, softened the lines of furnishings that were functional, but never utilitarian.

▲ *In the same room, a train frieze adds a final Early American touch, and frames the riot of color and pattern created by the patchwork quilts, above. Although the imagery in the frieze is unmistakably modern, its simple innocence refers directly to the stenciled designs that adorned early American walls.*

◀ *A colorful patchwork of quilts on seating, pillows, and shelves sets the tone for this reinterpreted Early American–style nursery, left. Other period design elements, such as the spindle crib, a hand-stenciled footstool and toy chest, and an old-fashioned wooden stick-toy and woolly sheep, mix comfortably with the contemporary storage unit.*

Today's Early American–style nursery follows the simple, clean lines of its historical model, whether the elements used are antiques, reproductions, contemporary interpretations, or plain classics. Furnishings, in pine or dark wood, tend to be limited to the essentials—a cane or plank-seat child's chair, perhaps stenciled or hand-painted with delicate farmyard motifs, flowers, or ABCs; a tiny painted footstool; a Boston rocker for mother, a scaled-down version for baby, even a doll's cradle; a heavy oak-panelled cradle, hooded to keep out drafts, and lined in simple cotton, or a Pennsylvania Dutch cradle, decorated with painted or stenciled hex signs or floral patterns and cutout, heart-shaped handholes; a pencil-post bed or crib; and a pine dresser.

Though functional, these furnishings are warm and welcoming. Moreover, the spareness and honesty inherent in their design and construction leaves plenty of scope for additional decoration in the Early American–style nursery. A sturdy folk-grained Pennsylvania dower chest serves as a toy chest or stores baby linens; an antique patchwork quilt, too delicate to be used, hangs on the wall above a crib; a rustic kindling box holds stuffed animals. Other details that lend period character to today's Early American nurseries include fanlight windows, four-panelled wooden doors with metal doorlatches, traditional needlepoint samplers or wood-framed reproductions of early American farm scenes, and antique, painted tin candleboxes for keeping diaper pins or trinkets.

Perhaps the most notable feature of Early American style is the use of stencils to create rhythmic painted patterns on walls, floors, and furnishings. Ironically, the art of stenciling, now being revived for its naive charm, represented the beginnings of mass-produced home decoration in eighteenth-century America.

With a limited range of pigments and a kit of hand-cut stencils, itinerant artisans transformed small, dark rooms with dark wood floors and uneven plaster walls into friendly, colorful environments. Though often only the most important, public rooms in the houses were stenciled, these decorated rooms were evidently a delight to the children as much as to the adults. One woman interviewed in the 1930s by Janet Waring for her now-classic book *Early American Stencil Designs* (1937; reprinted in

▲ *The Early American weathervane in a boy's room, above, aims an arrow in the direction of the light-diffusing lace panel, which covers the window in simple, Early American style. Beneath the window a hand-cut and -painted cowboy customizes the wooden chest, splitting in half to allow access to the drawers.*

▶ *Rustic and period elements, such as the turquoise-stained chest of drawers with brass hardware, the bird feeder, a ceramic sheep lamp base, and cutout goose wall plaque, soften this updated Early American–style nursery, right, with its plain crib and contemporary grid wallpaper.*

▲ *A play corner populated by handmade dolls dressed in calico is outfitted with an overturned basket and painted wooden tulips hand-cut in the Early American fashion, above. A rag rug, a chain of soft-sculpture gingerbread boys and hearts (a common symbol in American folk art), and a hanging quilt complete the warm and homey Early American–style atmosphere.*

◄ *Sunlight filtering through gauzy tiebacks into this farmhouse-yellow nursery, left, emphasizes the charm of a gentle reinterpretation of Early American design features. The rustic wicker bassinet can be wheeled to the window to catch morning rays. Old-fashioned pull- and stick-toys lie ready for play on an Early American–style rag rug.*

1968) remembered as a child counting the brightly stenciled wall figures as a favorite game. Another woman recalled the occasional thrill of being allowed to climb up and down the adults' front stairway, with its yellow and green stenciled stars and sunbursts.

Typical Early American stencil motifs included hearts and bells, starflowers, sunbursts, festoons, vines, wicker baskets, and willows. Colors, applied to plain or color-washed plastered walls, tended to be somewhat subdued, and were generally limited to red and rose, blues, and greens. The individuality of the designs resulted from unique combinations of motifs, for, as Waring wrote, "a flower head could be attached to almost any spray of foliage, while a heart, a rayed disc, or circle could be placed as an accent of color on a stem or in the center of a geometric pattern."

Many eighteenth-century stencil designs have been recovered and are being reproduced in today's nurseries whether as friezes, borders, or allover designs. Floors, too, are being decorated with stencil designs as they were in early American days—at the time, creating durable, economical substitutes for the painted canvas floorcloths or patterned carpetings that were becoming fashionable.

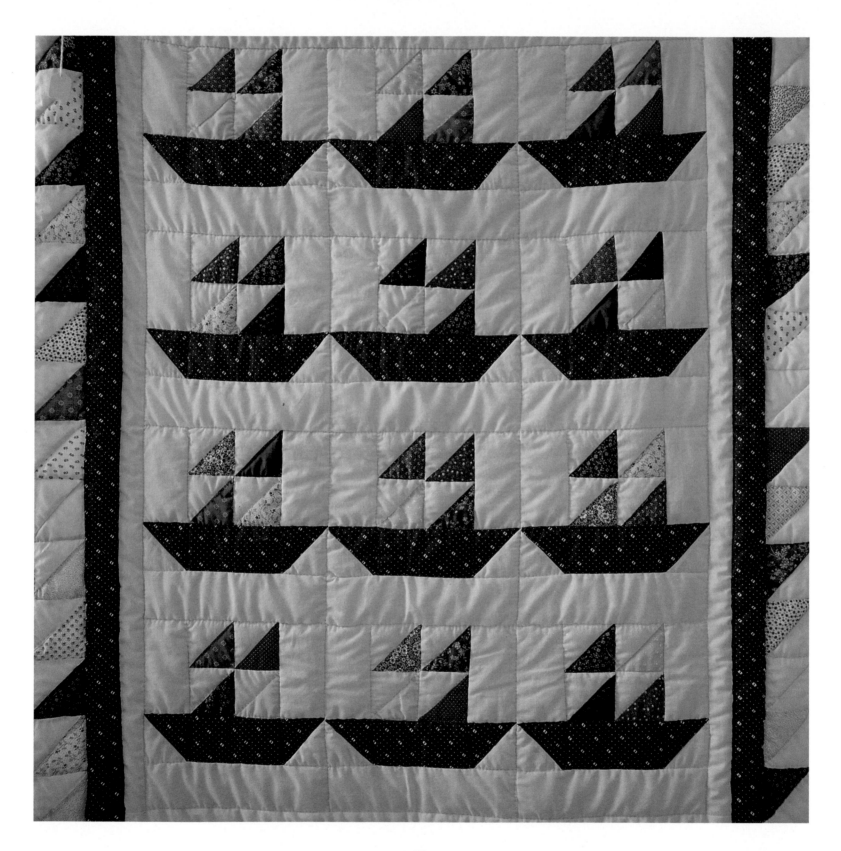

▲ *Raggedy Ann and Raggedy Andy are contemporary popularizations of the traditional American rag doll, above. Rag or wooden dolls were made at home from scraps or rags and leftover yarn and their faces were painted, often crudely, by hand. They were and still are much-loved toys for both boys and girls.*

◀ *Quilts — whether purchased or made specially for the nursery by a loved one or a group of friends at a quilting bee/baby shower — are delightful additions to a child's room decorated in the Early American tradition. This ship pattern, left, pieced together from fabric cut into triangles and squares, provides hours of enjoyment as a baby or small child looks at the pleasing repetition of the fleet of boats where no two sails are quite alike.*

▲ *Quilts displaying figures from nursery rhymes, such as the Calico Cat and the Gingham Dog, hanging on the wall, above, can provide a focus for a nursery decorating scheme. Soft sculptures of stars and moons in matching prints can be hung on the wall, in a window, or over the crib. Dolls with soft clothes, hair, and simple faces can add a charming touch and become a small child's first companions.*

VICTORIAN

The elaborate, flamboyant style developed in the nineteenth century by the Victorians has become a popular design style in today's nursery, a turn of the tide after decades during which all progressive design efforts were aimed at ridding the nursery of what was considered Victorian style's overabundant fussiness. There are several reasons for the popularity of Victorian-style nurseries, not least being the growing trend toward restoring, rather than modernizing, period homes.

Perhaps the main attraction of the Victorian nursery is that it belongs to an era remembered as something of a golden age for children, compared at least to the harsh rigors of the typical seventeenth- or eighteenth-century childhood. This was the era that began to redefine childhood as a tender period of awakening. In fact, the nursery as we know it today — a place designed for the nurture of the young, just as seedlings are gently tended in nursery gardens — can be said to have its origin in the nineteenth-century home. Houses of the growing middle class were now large enough to afford separate rooms for children, and the wealthiest families could even pay a live-in baby nurse who, of course, had her own room as well.

The Victorian child was cherished and indulged with material things. In this new age of industrialized mass production, items for the home were suddenly and widely affordable; and for the first time, all kinds of things were being produced specifically for children and their nurseries — a huge and profitable market. No sooner had children's book illustration come into its own as an art form than the work of the century's most popular illustrators — Kate Greenaway, Randolph Caldecott, and Walter Crane — was being adapted for nursery wallpapers and accessories. Nursery furnishings were produced in every style imaginable, toys of tin or wood and mechanical novelties proliferated, the concept of educational toys such as alphabet or building blocks was introduced, and china dolls graced the shelves of little girls. When P. T. Barnum ordered a child-sized set of walnut furniture made for Tom Thumb, consis-

▲ *This antique child's washbasin is decorated with figures based on Kate Greenaway characters, above. In today's Victorian-style room its function is decorative, except as an occasional bathtub for bears.*

▶ *In this Victorian-inspired nursery, right, scaled-down white wicker chairs are complemented by hand-painted ribbon-and-bow motifs on the walls, folding screen, and tabletop. A small collection of silver and ceramic jars and a vase lends a final period touch.*

▲ *The Victorian garden theme is reinterpreted in this nursery, above, with antique white wicker chair and desk, mailbox pencil holder, a russet-colored wreath, and a plaster column topped with tumbling English ivy. Wallpaper strewn with pink flowers complements the pink and white stripe of the chair pillow.*

◀ *A highly ornate wicker chair and ottoman, with pillows covered in delicate floral fabric to match the wallpaper, nudge up against sturdy bookshelves to create a cozy Victorian-style nook, left, for nursing or reading fairy tales.*

ting of a sofa, two armchairs, two side chairs, and a rocking chair, several specially made duplicate sets were sold to indulgent Victorian parents.

Yet it is not only objects, but also a particular sensibility that characterizes Victorian style and makes it particularly appropriate for the nursery. "Home, sweet home" was a cocoon—warm, soft, enclosing, and filled with objects of sentiment. Comfort—physical, emotional, and visual—was paramount. In the words of Jane Austen's Emma, "Ah! There is nothing like staying home for real comfort." Edges and corners were rounded with wood trim or fabrics were thrown over them; seats were overstuffed, bedding was plump with feathers.

Just as Victorian prudery demanded that bodies be covered from head to toe, so the Victorian interior was preserved from any suggestion of bareness. Floors, tables, walls, windows, and ceilings were covered with at least one layer of fabric, paper, or matting.

Combined with the Victorian love for pattern, this layered-on detail of interior surfaces resulted in an extravagance of pattern on pattern, of many colors and textures, and abundant motifs large and small—just the kind of visual stimulation on which babies apparently thrive. At its best, the effect could be sumptuously cozy, especially when light colors and patterns were chosen. It could be dressy at the same time, as in the case of a nursery designed for a New Jersey family in the 1890s, with its flowered chintz tieback door curtains (which served as draft excluders) and matching mantelpiece skirt.

"A white wall is always appropriate for lavatories and pigsties," wrote the nineteenth-century wallpaper designer Christopher Dresser. The visual intricacy of the Victorian interior with its allover patterns, its wainscoting and cornices, its Gothic-inspired, heavily leaded and often colored windowpanes, its chintzes and tassels and bows and frills, was considered not only decorative but also beneficial to the character and therefore especially important for children growing up amidst the ugliness of the industrial revolution. Those without access to wallpaper pasted children's book illustrations on the nursery wall.

Faced with an expanding world that yielded an unprecedented choice of styles and products, the Victorians decorated their homes eclectically, and often excessively. As

▲ *Victorian-style lace curtains and ruffled crib bedding with ribbon ties mingle with contemporary wall stenciling and colors in this pretty nursery, above. The weathered window box, with its narcissi, links the two distinct styles.*

masters of mix and match, they created not one, but many revival styles, sometimes combining elements from any number of stylistically diverse periods, Gothic to Romanesque. Even sets of children's building blocks were made in a number of different architectural styles.

Today's Victorian-style nursery tends to avoid the heavy opulence and overabundance of certain Victorian interiors, emulating instead the lighter, airy side of Victoriana while creating a peaceful sense of soft and faded charm. It is an atmosphere typically created not with nursery sets, but with a diverse collection of furnishings and accessories that might have been handed down through the generations: a white-painted wicker bassinet or crib, probably canopied, that may have been caned in the village shop, flanked by a wicker chair, rocker, and settee, perhaps scaled-down, or a white-enameled, curvilinear brass crib or bedstead—all dressed in eyelet and lace that grandmother might have made as she sat rocking under a gaslight, or thrown over with cushions embroidered with moral instruction on a quiet Sunday afternoon. Wall and ceiling papers, in soft colors reminiscent of dried flowers and printed with tiny floral patterns or with delicately

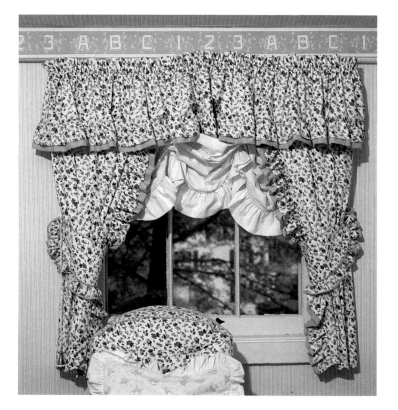

▲ *Striped cotton festoon blinds peek out from behind floral tiebacks and a generous valance, adding to the layered pattern-on-pattern effect that lends this tiny nursery its Victorian cottage charm, above.*

◀ *New and antique pieces live happily together in a girl's Victorian-style bedroom, left. Next to the wicker-headed bed, an antique white wicker nightstand holds a potted plant, and a pair of decorative wooden rabbits nestle under a wall-mounted, gardenlike wreath.*

lettered ABCs, may be layered over with faded photos of distant ancestors or with old letters elaborately penned in ink, framed in gilt, perhaps even matted with paper doilies. Posies of small flowers from the garden or wildflowers picked in the hedgerows, with names like honesty, sweet william, or everlasting, link the nursery with the garden that was so dear to the Victorian heart, while a window seat serves for quiet reading and contemplation of the world.

There is, on the other hand, a more vibrant and sturdy style in Victorian nurseries that many see as more appropriate for boys. This kind of nursery draws attention to the Victorian era as an age of invention and discovery. It may feature wall and ceiling papers printed with sailing ships or steam trains; P. T. Barnum circus posters from the nineteenth century; displays of painted tin mechanical toys or vehicles; a wooden rocking or hobbyhorse; an antique Victorian child's chair, with cutout and painted side supports in the shape of a horse or dog.

In the Victorian-style nursery, storage and display problems are solved in a way that small children can truly appreciate. For, just as the toddler returns from successive outings clutching found stones or leaves, or odd scraps of paper, so the Victorians gathered small, personally meaningful knickknacks over a period of time. And just as small children delight in sorting their little mementos according to some random system of classification, so the Victorians arranged their knickknacks in small displays by size, or color, or shape on little shelves in Victorian corner "whatnots," or window ledges and mantels. In the Victorian-style nursery, a small shelf edged with gingerbread trim may hold a display of old wooden pull-toys, or a collection of favorite round rocks; a mantel might hold a miniature village scene made with one of the wooden building sets that were intended to build the character of the nineteenth-century child, or display a collection of seashells gathered on vacation.

Dollhouses and dolls' cradles, miniature log cabins, hobbyhorses, and tiny china tea sets—these kinds of toys were nursery props for children's make-believe. Whatever the interpretation of Victorian style for children, its nursery-rhyme innocence reflects an era that understood the child's need for a special imaginary world that, on a simple level, reflected the world of the grown-ups.

▶ *A white enameled, cast iron crib with brass accents, a matching changing table with heart-shaped curlicues, and a commodious wicker rocking chair are all it takes to transform a modern, city nursery, right, into an updated Victorian setting. With its closet wall and built-in window shelf and storage unit, this efficient nursery is designed to grow along with the child.*

▼ *In an all gold and white nursery, a modern window is transformed by a romantic, Victorian-inspired vignette, below. China fashion dolls were prized possessions in the nineteenth-century home. Here, bride and groom are flanked by a line of dancing china ballerinas on one side, and on the other by a ruffled and heart-shaped picture frame. The flounced window shade, custom-made in a tiny gold on white print, serves to soften the edges of the window frame while admitting a gently diffused daylight.*

▲ *The ribbon-and-bow motif that encircles the walls of this nursery, above, was popular in Victorian times. Here, trompe l'oeil shadows and Alice in Wonderland scale make it a strictly contemporary interpretation. The Victorian theme is continued in the wicker furnishings. The lamp and hamper were hand-painted and beribboned to coordinate with the wall decoration.*

▶ *A graceful vignette created on this wide window shelf and framed by tieback, fringed drapes gives the nursery, right, an old-fashioned charm. Window light passing through a goldfish bowl shimmers on the polished silver surfaces of heirloom cups, piggy banks, and a teether.*

ENGLISH STYLE

"The Englishman builds his house for himself alone," said the German writer Herman Muthesius in *The English House* (1904), the book that defined for our century the character of English domestic architecture and life. The English house, Muthesius wrote, is an intensely private domain, a sanctuary in which traditional life-styles may continue undisturbed, and classbound values may be preserved in the face of upheavals brought about by commerce, industry, and changing fashions.

Even in the homes of the English upper classes, a certain amount of stylistic understatement is interpreted as a sign of nobility. For, Muthesius pointed out, the Englishman shuns "a showy architecture that draws attention to itself . . . style with a capital S." In English style, as in English manners, ostentation is considered in bad taste, and good taste is less a matter of evident style than of evident grace, characterized by a quality that is unassuming, low key, and respectful of tradition — family tradition, cultural tradition, and the history of the house itself.

▶ *This city playroom, right, is decorated with latticework and hand-painted, trompe l'oeil wisteria in the style of an English country garden. Stone columns were painted on either side of an existing dark gray marble fireplace, which is offset by the light garden furniture near the window.*

Spurred on perhaps by a climate of desolately gray skies, the English have created a style that manages to transform large, nobly proportioned interiors into warm, intimate environments that reflect the lives of those who live in them. Rooms, for all their fine architectural detailing, tend to be focused on the hearth — even today homes are generally built with fireplaces — with its hearth rug, its fire screen, an often ornate fire surround, a set of iron pokers and tongs for tending the coal fire and toasting bread, and the all-important mantelpiece. Draft excluders, often decorative or whimsical, stop the cold that creeps in under closed doors. The climate, and the national love for pictorial decoration, may also explain a two-hundred-year fascination in England for wallpapers, an important ingredient of English style.

Above all this is a style, seemingly uncomposed, made of individual furnishings and objects of value, family possessions that may have been passed down through generations. Furnishings are typically large-scale and heavy — chests, tables, and wardrobes expertly crafted from old oak; high bedsteads of wood, brass, or iron; large, plumply upholstered and sprung armchairs and sofas, simply skirted, that have survived countless misadventures and children's children. English style tends toward a faded gentility, in which comfort and use are seen as the most sensible, and therefore the most worthwhile priorities. The nursery in particular is a room decorated in a sensible, though by no means austere, manner, with frills and lace used only as unobtrusive accents.

English style is far from being a country style. Yet, whether it is found in a city apartment or a country mansion, it is eminently liveable, perhaps because it has absorbed many features of the English country house and of the countryside itself. The motifs and images that recur in so many English rooms are those of an almost parklike, tamed countryside, a countryside of small meadows, of gently rolling hills and winding lanes. The flowers that dot the wallpaper and run over the upholstery range from tiny meadow wildflowers like buttercups or forget-me-nots, to roses, historically the flower of England, and honeysuckle trailing over a trellis. And the animals that decorate the nursery are, like the animals of Beatrix Potter's tales, small and friendly inhabitants of the English fields and farm-

▲ *Antique, decorative wall shelves embellished with roses, and a sepia-toned print showing children at play in an English village, are hung on walls papered in an understated pink stripe for a truly English look, above.*

◄ *Illusion and reality mingle peacefully in a pastoral scene inspired by the English countryside, left. The trompe l'oeil meadows and hamlet, thrown into relief by painted-on trellising, serve as a backdrop to a vase of tulips and a treasured collection of horses.*

yards—rabbits, squirrels, geese, ducks, sparrows, lambs, and field mice. These animals, which may be painted onto furnishings or walls, used to embellish nursery tea sets, or propped on mantelpiece or bed in the form of ceramic figurines or stuffed animals, represent that softness of the English countryside so clearly expressed in the English-style nursery.

The English-style palette is generally soft, like that of the watercolors that represent England's favorite amateur art form. Like the naturalistic motifs central to the English decorative tradition, these colors owe much to the colors of the countryside. Whites tend to be creamy, and yellows buttery. Pinks are seldom stronger than faded rose, or apple blossom. Lilac and lavender, which grow rampant through the countryside, are frequent bedroom colors. Blues tend to be used in delicate, bird's egg shades, while green, whether light or dark, is generally mossy.

The decorative elements of English style have been enriched by influences from abroad during Britain's years of Empire and sea trade. From India and the Orient come wicker furnishings, ceramic forms like ginger jars, and Oriental area rugs, as well as countless motifs and patterns from Turkey and Persia. The rocking chair, from America, has been transformed into the gliding, or platform, rocker, which may be part of an upholstered set.

Interpretations of English style for the nursery are subtly varied. The Welsh-born designer Laura Ashley has created a pretty, cottagelike English style, for both children and adults, derived from English country. The work and influence of Victorian illustrator Kate Greenaway, whose prim but delicate and highly decorative drawings have adorned all things for children since they were first published in the late 1800s, continues to find a place in the English-style nursery. Some less prettified interpretations take their cues from the grander English homes, with large areas of wall divided into panels by moldings or chair and picture rails, or covered in subtly striped papers. In this style of nursery, beds are often covered with candlewick bedspreads, and chairs are upholstered in chintz or tapestry-like fabrics.

Whatever the interpretation, the English-style nursery is likely to include a few quintessentially English accessories, typically things related to the life of the individual family.

▶ *A diverse assortment of repainted and reupholstered antique furnishings, together with ample room proportions and fine architectural detailing, give this girl's bedroom, right, the comfortable and live-in feeling that is central to English style. Dusty blue accents on the desk and chair echo the color of the curtains' ribbon motif. The pink bow painted onto the wastebasket is repeated in the extravagant bow ties of the tapestry chair pillow. The children's rooms in this house were all inspired by English watercolors the client supplied to the designer as source material.*

▲ *A delicate trompe l'oeil rendition of a flower-encircled bird feeder at the top of the staircase that leads to the playroom, above, was based on pictures found in English garden books and children's literature.*

◀ *This English-style bedroom, left, features an antique iron bed with matching dolls' cot, a scattering of English prints and watercolors, and lamps with beribboned shades.*

The walls, whether painted or papered, may be scattered with watercolors of the English countryside or seaside; with framed watercolor illustrations from a favorite Beatrix Potter book or some other story that has been read for at least two generations; or with the botanical sketches that have long been a specialty of English artists.

A stuffed Paddington Bear, in Wellington boots and sou'wester, is a suitable guest in any English-style nursery. A doll's perambulator, the bulky, English variety with closed sides to prevent drafts, is standard girls' fare and a useful place to keep a collection of dolls or stuffed animals. Portraits of family pets — cats and dogs especially — are characteristically English. And anything to do with horses, from pictures of ponies or hunting scenes, to horse brasses or bright colored rosettes won by young riders at country gymkhanas, has a special place on English bedroom walls. The mantelpiece might hold a coronation cup, or a Bunnykins china tea set by Royal Doulton.

Perhaps the most English of nursery images is the fairy. Whether it is the gossamer-winged Tinkerbell of Peter Pan, a flower fairy from Cicely Barker's *Flower Fairy Picture Books*, or the mischievous pixies, gnomes, or elves of Arthur Rackham's art, these characters are firmly entrenched in English folklore and cannot fail to add romance to the English-style nursery.

▲   *The recessed and raised "gazebo" with painted-on latticework, above, was designed as a games area, with uncarpeted floor. The trompe l'oeil English country landscape that sweeps around all three walls makes this a favorite spot for dollhouse fantasy play, under the watchful gaze of a ceramic, reclining marmalade cat.*

▶   *Classically English vignettes of garden and domestic scenes with animal characters, based on tales by Beatrix Potter, are framed into panels defined by modified, eighteenth-century stencil patterns of leaves and flowers, right.*

POSTMODERN

Starting out as a loosely defined movement in architecture and the arts, postmodernism grew out of an opposition to the theories of functional modernism that gave us "dumb boxes" to live in, and to notions of "good design" as something functional, clean lined, and sensible.

Central to postmodernism is the idea that design, while using the most advanced materials and techniques available, must acknowledge people's psychological need for humor, warmth, and meaningful shapes, colors, and forms. Design is a language that, if used to its full potential, can be stimulating, comforting, and capable of triggering a flow of association. "Less is a bore," wrote architect Robert Venturi in answer to Ludwig Mies van der Rohe's modernist "less is more" edict banning decoration and ornamentation in architecture and design.

During the 1980s postmodern established itself as a mainstream design style fusing various threads of architectural postmodernism with a measure of pop culture. The result is a look that is fresh, playful, colorful, and quirky, yet fundamentally elegant and sophisticated in its witty visual puns. The childlike quality of much postmodern styling, its decorative use of color combined with its inventive approach to practical, modern materials, has made it increasingly popular in the nursery, where its more amusing and fanciful qualities have been emphasized.

Postmodern design is the style of a consumer culture with choice. It plunders the past, the present, the globe, for stylistic fragments that can be fused into a new, articulate whole. It draws on and mixes different elements from history, but does not copy them. Instead, features from different periods and places are borrowed to be whimsically reinterpreted and stylized, often to the point of cartoonlike exaggeration: a "chair rail" painted straight onto the wall and accented with bold zigzags, turning a traditionally functional feature into a purely decorative device; plywood cut, shaped, and installed to resemble fanciful exposed farmhouse roof beams; crosshatching,

▲ *The unusual, custom-built storage unit, above, is a sophisticated and practical solution for an older child's room. Its architectural styling with pediment and "room" shelves gives it a postmodern flavor.*

▲ *The upper turret area of a postmodern "castle" room, above, doubles as a lookout tower and a passage to the loftlike sleeping area. Ramparts make the raised level safe.*

▲ *This architect-designed child's chair, complete with pitched roof and chimney backrest, is both humorous and practical, above. Laminated in solid-core Formica, it is made for wear and tear; its widely spaced, building-block–like legs give it extra stability.*

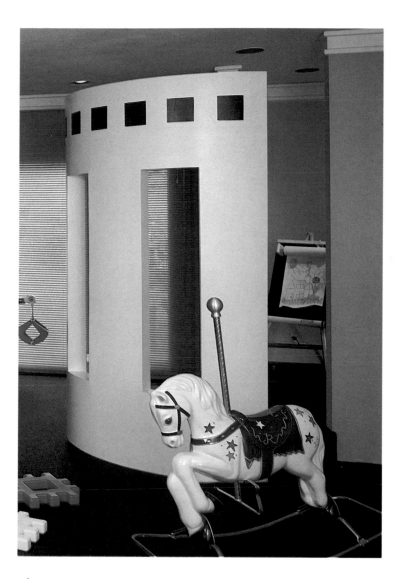

▲ *A freestanding screen wall, with light-admitting cut-outs, separates areas in postmodern style, above. Behind the wall is a quiet area for painting and drawing. On the other side, a gliding horse recalls the fun of the carousel.*

◄ *A postmodern, architectural storage unit lends a witty quality to this nursery, left, and provides a strong incentive for children to tidy up possessions.*

borrowed from artists' sketchbooks and blown up to make a pattern for crib or bed linens.

Themes and materials from different sources are often combined in the most surprising ways: a child's Windsor chair, for instance, painted a metallic blue and stenciled in a pattern derived from computer graphics; a "Victorian" pedestal table whose laminate top looks like a fried egg; or a corner shelf styled in the form of a paper cutout palm tree. Faux finishes, not necessarily deceptive, are also reinterpreted for the present. The postmodern crib may simply be a standard wooden crib that has been painted in a hot pink marbleized finish.

Architecture itself, and especially the typical shape of the postmodern house facade, is an often repeated motif in postmodern design. In the nursery: crib styles with architecturally arched head- and footboards, a storage unit shaped like the scaled-down facade of a skyscraper, house-shaped bookends, a house-shaped room divider, a blue kidney-shaped rug that looks like a suburban swimming pool and at the same time recalls a familiar 1950s shape.

Although a certain amount of postmodern nursery furniture is mass-produced, the postmodern nursery often features elements that have been custom-made or adapted from adult designs. A traditional rolltop desk, for instance, refinished in a speckled composition-book pattern and used as a changing table; large cartoon-character shapes cut out of the doors of a plain armoire, or even out of a plasterboard wall, and the shapes filled with colored Plexiglas; or the top of a plasterboard knee wall cut to resemble medieval fortifications.

Inspired by fast-food roadside architecture as much as by classical harmonies and Victorian eclecticism, postmodern design tends to play with scale and structure as it does with architectural motifs, often giving the postmodern children's room an Alice in Wonderland quality in which many children delight.

2 Nursery Color

▲ *Colors are most intensified against a gray background, above. The bright colors of oversized crayons and vividly painted wood trim pop out against a soft gray wall and window shade.*

Babies see color before they see form. Contrary to previous belief, research findings suggest that a newborn still in the delivery room not only responds to, but is attracted by moving, bright colors within the baby's very short focusing range. Farther away, color is reduced to brightness and darkness, until the baby has lost its natural newborn near-sightedness. Hanging mobiles and crib bedding with strong color contrasts may be the infant's first forms of real color stimulation.

The quest for stimulating sensations continues as the baby learns to grab at brightly colored objects. But in the meantime, connections are being made between colors and things. By the age of three or four children may combine a firm sense of color preference — typically clear, bright hues — with a rudimentary form of personal color association. A preschooler will still choose by color, perhaps picking to sit in an uncomfortable yellow chair rather than a comfortable brown one, but the choice of color will be a more complex one than previously. The intense, idealized, childish response to color sensations is a poignant feature of the nursery years; it is short-lived. Yet, perhaps because it is so significant in early life, color remains the first line of communication when it comes to decorating the home, and the nursery in particular.

In the nursery, as in the rest of the home, the choice of palette depends on a number of interrelated factors. Sometimes a range of colors is derived from a historical or regional style — Mediterranean colors, Early American colors, forties or fifties colors. Often nursery colors are chosen by more personal preferences. Since attraction to visual material is often based on personal color preferences, some or all of the colors from a favorite painting or children's book illustration, be it Beatrix Potter or van Gogh, may serve as inspiration for a palette. Sometimes a special toy chest or impulsively chosen wallpaper will give color cues for the rest of the room.

Today, there are no rules regarding the nursery palette, because we no longer consider infants to be fragile creatures whose excitable tendencies must be soothed in soft, pastel environments. Whether colors are to be delicate or strong will depend in part on how calming or stimulating the baby's environment is intended to be. Whether the colors are light or dark will depend on the size and proportions of the nursery. Whether the main color interest is to be on wall surfaces, furnishings, or curtains and bedding will depend on what kind of a nursery it is to be. Some designers feel that nursery walls should serve as a neutral background to the riot of colors that children's toys represent. Others feel that children can never have too much color, and that a wide range of hues is both stimulating and educative. Color gives the nursery its character, and that character is a reflection of one's vision of childhood.

▲ *Simple but bright walls and trim make an effective backdrop for the multicolored rag basket and an array of soft bears in several solid hues, above.*

▲ *Many designers prefer a neutral background to set off furnishings of bright colors. In this nursery, above, gray walls and a dark-colored carpet allow the intensity of primary-colored toys to give the room its color accents.*

WHAT IS RED?

"Mr. Rabbit," said the little girl, *"I want help."*

So begins a journey through the child's world of color — the subject of *Mr. Rabbit and the Lovely Present,* Charlotte Zolotow's 1962 children's story illustrated by Maurice Sendak, about a very small girl who wants to give her mother a birthday present, something she would really like. But what?

"She likes red," said the little girl.
"Red," said Mr. Rabbit. *"You can't give her red."*
"Something red, maybe," said the little girl.
"Oh, something red," said Mr. Rabbit.

Color, as Mr. Rabbit knows, is nothing more than a sensation. Favorite colors are only favorite retinal stimulations caused by light waves of different lengths reflecting off surfaces. Red, blue, yellow, or pink are abstract entities, names given to a number of related physiological experiences that are shared by humans, reptiles, fish, and birds, but not by most lower mammals. Dogs and cats, for instance, have no sensation of color; they see the world in tones of gray. Babies, on the other hand, meet the world through all of their senses, and their first and most powerful visual sensations after black and white are colors. As far as we know, infants not only see colors, but taste, feel, and hear them too.

▶ *Humpty Dumpty stripes and Harlequin diamonds enliven the fireplace, which doubles as a media center in this nursery, right. Traditional nursery rhyme characters such as these life-sized, handcrafted and -painted figures are opportunities for the addition of many primaries to white or muted color schemes.*

"What is red?" said the little girl.
"Well," said Mr. Rabbit, "there's red underwear."

There are also, he tells her, red roofs, red birds, red fire engines, and red apples. "Good," said the little girl. "That's good. She likes apples." We experience color only through the perceivable things in our world: grass, skin, walls, apples. Without form, or light to see it by, there is no color. But, in a world filled with light and forms of every kind, we can never have names enough for the millions of different colors that exist.

Though one speaks of red as an idea, the many rednesses of an apple are entirely different from the redness of a roof. Maria Montessori, a pioneer in modern early childhood education, believed that sensitivity to the nuances of color was essential to the growth of a person's creative intelligence, and can best be developed during the sensory, early years. In Montessori nursery schools today, toddlers are given "sensorial exercises," in which they play with materials providing "contrasted sensations," such as red and blue bricks, or "graded sensations," such as bricks in many shades of blue. As the eye becomes educated it is able to distinguish between, to work with, and to enjoy increasing numbers of colors, just as the trained ear can hear and use all the gradations in a tonal scale, and can distinguish between a note made by a piano and the same note made by a violin.

Color has often been spoken of as a kind of musical language, in which the colorist is a composer orchestrating symphonies that can, through harmony or discord, balance or contrast, convey moods, feelings, and meanings. The understanding and use of color is both a science and an art, and humans are born with both a physiological capacity to distinguish between lengths of light waves, and with an intense hunger for the aesthetic and emotional pleasures that these light waves can bring.

◀ *A riot of color turns a nursery for two, left, into a fantasy land. The saturated hues of the wall mural, which encircles the room with rolling green hills, summer blue sky, and anthropomorphic sun and flowers, balance with the primary-colored "house" beds and animal chairs, and with the green floor to create a complete, picture-book image of happy village life.*

PERCEPTION OF COLOR

"What is yellow?" said the little girl.

Scientifically, yellow is a physical sensation. But the experience of color is also a complex psychological event. Color, being abstract, tends to be associated with things — like red apples, the yellow sun, the color of a favorite dress — and things resonate with meaning, whether on a universal, cultural, or specifically personal level. Though colors have qualities that are universally recognized, such as the energy of red or the calm of blue or green, it is the personal factor that many consider to be the most important in color appreciation. Rorschach, famous for his ink blot personality tests, found that people who tend to control their emotions prefer the cool blues and greens, and avoid red.

People in all cultures have sought ways to communicate through a decorative art of applied color. From the earliest times, pigments were applied to the surfaces of walls, fabrics, pots, and other household items. Humans have painstakingly extracted, ground, and mixed colors from plants, animals, and minerals — yellow from pomegranate or the pistils of saffron; purple from lichen or from shellfish feeding off the coasts of Crete and Tyre; red from madder root and scarlet from the dry, powdered body of *Kermes*, an oriental louse; green from oxidized copper; blue from azurite. The ancient Peruvians found and produced pigments for almost 150 different colors. But traditionally color choices were often determined less by aesthetics than by magical theories and social or family traditions. The word *decorative* did not come into common use until 1791, shortly after the word *industrial* became popular.

In the mid-1800s chemical processes for producing pigments were introduced, and today vinyl tiles alone are produced in a range of one thousand colors. Magic no longer plays a conscious role in the decorative arts, and even the long-standing social tradition of the pastel nursery has become an option in style. Today the individual using color as an art of communication is working with several languages at once: a scientific language that in-cludes the chemistry of pigment; a symbolic language; the language of aesthetics as it is affected by personal factors, fashion, and historical reference; and a language of feeling — warm, cold, heavy, happy — that is the fusion of all the others. Everyone feels the effect of color. But babies and small children feel it most of all.

The scientific language of color begins with Newton who, in his 1704 work *Optiks*, showed for the first time that white light is made up of seven spectral colors — the rainbow of colors in a child's paintbox. Thomas Young, the scientist and Egyptologist who helped to translate the Rosetta stone, discovered what has become every child's first color lesson — that each color visible in the spectrum can be produced by a mixture of the three pure or primary colors — red, yellow, and blue.

As color emerged from the world of mystery and magic into the world of rational thought, theorists began to produce scales showing the interrelation of colors and how pigments can be identified, blended, and harmonized. The color wheel is the most rudimentary system; the most famous is Munsell's scale, or color tree, which categorizes color in its three interlocking dimensions — hue, intensity, and value, the core of the color language.

▶ *The color scheme in this pretty, yet simple, nursery, right, is composed of several custom-mixed shades that are related by similar values — clear colors mixed with a generous amount of white. Bright yet light, these gender-neutral colors combine to create a sunny effect reminiscent of Caribbean island style.*

HUE

"She likes green," said the little girl.

When one speaks of a favorite color, be it lime green or violet, one is speaking of a hue. Hues are actual colors as they appear in the spectrum. These include the three primary colors, secondary colors like orange made by mixing two primaries, and tertiary colors like blue-green, which can be made by mixing a primary with a secondary.

Hues range in warmth from the hottest, red, to the coldest, blue. And each hue has its own complement, the color that perfectly balances it. Violet, for instance, complements yellow, and blue-green complements orange-red. Since the eye seeks out such balances, always looking for a unified whole, even tiny highlights of a complementary color can be aesthetically pleasing. By thinking of color in terms of hue — how much yellow is in a particular red, how much blue is in a pink, or green in a blue — one can effectively relate and combine hues.

Equally as important as hue itself is its degree of saturation or intensity. A pure green is an intense color, but mixed with gray or blue it loses in intensity what it gains in subtlety. In interior design, hues are rarely used in their fully saturated forms, except for accents. Babies and small children, however, tend to prefer the most saturated hues — firetruck red, schoolbus yellow, toy blue.

Color is also characterized by value, its lightness or darkness. Some hues, like red, are naturally dark and absorbent in value, while others, like sky blue, are naturally light and reflective. In many primitive languages colors were referred to only as "light" or "dark"; there were no names for hues. The coordination and balancing of color is as much a matter of value as hue: light may be balanced against dark for contrast; or there may be a serene consistency of value; or darker colors like forest green may be placed low, and light colors like violet toward the ceiling, just as in nature the darkness of grass pales upward to the light sky. In terms of pigments, the lightness or darkness of a color is also determined by the extent to which it is mixed with black or white. A tint such as pink is a hue mixed with white; a shade like midnight blue is a hue mixed with black. Most commonly-used wall colors are, in fact, tints or shades.

Neanderthal man had pigments for only three hues and black, but by developing techniques ranging from simple finger painting and blowing paint through a hollow bird bone, to the use of mineral "crayons" and brushes of hair or fiber, he turned a primitive palette into an astonishing range of effects. Today designers and architects are rediscovering many decorative techniques for both mixing and applying pigments — glazing, stippling, sponging, pickling, and others — that were for many years considered old-fashioned, if not archaic. Stripped of convention, these techniques are often used playfully — a nursery dado marbleized in bubble gum pink, for instance. And by adding the "tactile" dimension of visual texture to the experience of color, such surface treatments have made that experience all the richer.

▶ *The dusky blue and aqua of the window dressings are echoed in the painted, trompe l'oeil cubes scattered over the walls, and in the processional frieze of rocking horses, right. A predominance of white, blue, and green, set off by yellow accents, gives this nursery a fresh, cool feeling.*

To apply color to surfaces in an interior setting is essentially to compose a colored image of the room, as an artist composes on canvas, whether color is embodied in pattern or solid, paint or paper, flooring, furnishing, or window treatments. Working with an understanding of hue, saturation, and value, the designer, like the painter, develops a "palette," or range of colors. The range may be wide or narrow, bright or subdued, harmonious or discordant. There are restrained, monochromatic schemes, in which one hue is used in various values — pink and burgundy for instance — or the more difficult but vibrant polychromatic schemes that contrast unrelated hues such as reds, yellows, and blues. Great paintings and illustrations are often explorations of the effects and interrelationships of colors, and as such are a frequent source of inspiration and ideas for the decorator's palette.

Rooms, like paintings, are composed of figure and background. The modern nursery from the 1950s on was characterized by plain walls and floors that formed a neutral ground for patterned fabrics on the bed and at the window. Today walls and furnishings may be grounds for pattern or decoration with stencil designs, murals, or decorative papers; or an attractive range of solid colors may become the decorative element. The walls may be subtly colored as background, with furnishings or colored moldings providing the accent; or the walls may hold the interest and detail, while the furnishings and other elements are restrained and low in color saturation. Sometimes, as in many Victorian nurseries, an allover feeling is achieved with walls, furnishings, drapes, and floor all of equal value and intensity.

Color also plays a dynamic structural role. Hues of a long wavelength, such as warm red, appear to be closer than hues of a short wavelength, like cool blue. Light colors, because they look airy, and cold colors, because they seem distant, tend to expand space. Warm and dark colors seem to pull the walls inward, making large rooms feel more intimate. The modernists' concern with structure led them to some serious investigations of color's spatial dynamics. Now that a free use of color has returned to the home, designers and architects are illusionistically raising and lowering ceilings, dividing and separating areas of rooms, and in every way restructuring space.

A restricted palette of grayed-down, solid shades defines areas and creates a serene atmosphere in an airy child's room, left. Carpeting, chair upholstery, and bed coverings repeat the dusty pink of the walls in a slightly stronger shade. The muted green of the wall defining the recessed sleeping area is picked up in the green of the sofa. A scattering of throw pillows covered in a green and pink print, and a well-dressed green, pink, and creamy yellow frog unite the room's principal hues, while providing a needed focus for the eyes.

◀ *A predominantly pastel nursery, left, with pale yellow walls, matching yellow chaise lounge, and soft, blue-gray carpeting, is enlivened with the addition of white and bright accents. White-painted woodwork, including double doors, window frame, baseboard, crib, cloud-edged shelving, and table and chairs set, gives the room an airy feel, while bright yellow and red in the antique quilt, astronaut chair, and changing table pad introduce a childish element. The airplane picture on the wall and the yellow-backed parachute pillows on the chaise lounge pull together the various color themes, including the green of the large palm that graces the corner of the room.*

FEELING COLOR

"What is blue?" said the little girl.
"Lakes are blue," said Mr. Rabbit.

Colors can be evasive, fluctuating. They seem to change under the influence of surface texture and light. Just as a lake takes on the colors of sky and trees, making *lake blue* a nebulous term, so a table painted shiny blue takes on the yellow lamplight, the pink ceiling, the violet flowers. Different materials take color differently. The yellowness of a yellow plastic toy is not like the yellowness of dyed cotton or painted stucco, and each of these changes with the intensity and direction of the light.

Colors also appear to change in interaction with other colors. As John Ruskin, the English art critic, wrote toward the turn of the century, "Every hue . . . is altered by every touch that you add in other places," so that "what was in harmony when you left it, becomes discordant as you set other colors beside it," and what seemed light seems dark as you place it next to white. Sometimes a conflict between two opposing hues will be mysteriously reconciled by the addition of a third.

These objective qualities of color can be measured and predicted. But there is another, potent dimension that is intriguing precisely because it is unmeasurable and irrational—what has been called the "feeling dimension" of color. As Gyorgy Kepes wrote in *The Language of Vision* (1944), "We are able to see, or it appears that we are able to see, what the eye structurally is not capable of seeing. We see warm and cold, quiet and loud, sharp and dull, light and heavy, sad and gay, static and dynamic, wild and tame colors." In other words, we see in colors expressive qualities that are normally associated with our other senses. We see, hear, touch, and smell color. It is this "feeling dimension" of color that babies and small children are said to experience most powerfully.

Wassily Kandinsky, a leader of the German Expressionist movement Blue Rider before joining the Bauhaus, explored the relationships between color, sound, and feel-

▲ *Lamplight magically transforms the colors in a room—making some color schemes natural choices for rooms that do both day and night duty. In an inviting bedroom, above, pale, apricot-colored wallpaper patterned with white pinstripes and brighter motifs takes on the yellow glow of a lamp, as does the highly reflective, gold-colored lamp base.*

▶ *Dusty colors and custom paint effects give this city nursery, right, an old-fashioned flavor, which is echoed in framed prints reproduced from Cicely Barker's* Flower Fairy Picture Books. *Head- and footboard, designed to fit standard rails, were hand-painted with accents of grayed blue to match the stippled wall and bed linens. Hand-stenciled pinwheels on the bedside table are repeated in a frieze.*

ing in his highly influential work of 1946, *On the Spiritual in Art*. Like many of his contemporaries, Kandinsky had been searching for a way to use color abstractly in his paintings, so that pure hues, not familiar forms, would be the expressive medium. Color, he was convinced, has a life of its own, independent of the material world, and by understanding the emotional resonances and sensory impact of color, one can touch the deepest realms of the human spirit.

Kandinsky's convictions concerning color stemmed in part from his own childhood memories. "The first colors that made a strong impression on me were bright, juicy green, white, carmine red, black, and yellow ochre," he wrote in *Reminiscences* (1913). "These memories go back to the third year of my life. I saw these colors on various objects which are no longer as clear in my mind as the colors themselves." Kandinsky's investigations of hues were directed toward recapturing this powerful, childish, direct relationship to color—pure sensation combined with the most universal of emotions.

Like the little girl in the story who wanted to give her mother red, the young Kandinsky identified with the color itself, not with the object from which the color emanated. The first years of life are essentially sensation oriented and nonmaterialistic. This was demonstrated by an experiment in which children of various ages were asked to match a green triangle with either a green square or a red triangle. Without hesitation, the preschoolers chose the green square, ignoring shape in favor of the enormous appeal of color. Older children, on the other hand, chose the red triangle. They had already learned to think in terms of things, forms, and shapes.

Antique bed and bed linens combine with a classic pink, blue, and white color theme, and with old-fashioned, hand-painted ribbon-and-bow and flower motifs on walls and portable screen in this feminine child's room, left.

PASTELS

The word *pastel* comes from the French for a pigmented paste made into a crayonlike stick that is used by artists to color on heavily textured white paper. Though pastel crayons are fairly intense in color, the whiteness of the paper shows through and gives the impression of a pale, delicate color. In the language of design, pastel colors are tints of hues with low intensity and light value.

Hues become pastels as white is added, and in the process undergo radical transformations. The energy of red is dissipated as it is mixed with white to make pink; and the lighter the pink, the more it loses vibrancy and warmth and takes on the very different characteristics of white—openness, clarity, and to some people a kind of emptiness. Yet something of the hue's qualities always remain in a pastel. A pale, sky blue is always cooler than a peachy tint of orange; a light, mint green retains the calming nature of pure green; and a soft lavender exhibits the luminosity that characterizes its saturated parent hue, violet.

Because pastels lack intensity, yet are clear and unambiguous, they have long been considered the most suitable colors for the nursery. Babies in this culture have traditionally been considered vulnerable, delicate creatures, and until Dr. Spock revolutionized parenting with his views on the nature of babyhood, strong colors were thought to arouse the undesirable, animal instincts inherent in infants. The custom of choosing pale blue for a boy and pink for a girl is also strictly cultural. In France, for instance, blue is customarily associated with girls, in reference to the heavenly blue of the Virgin Mary's gown.

Though pastels are no longer the rule for babies, these pale colors are still favored for small nurseries because they have a light, airy feel and tend to give the impression of expanding space. Pale blue is the most expansive of the pastels, while a gentle yellow emphasizes the charm of a tiny sunlit room. In the small nursery, where simplicity is of the essence, pastels are often accented with white—white woodwork, white wicker, white crib and rocking chair, and perhaps white light-filtering drapes.

▶ *The wall becomes a canvas in this lyrical reinterpretation of the "pastel for babies" tradition, right. A stylized rainbow against a yellow sky repeats the arch of head- and footboard below, while the crisper edges of stenciled moon and stars enhance the illusion of depth. A soft white extends downward, cloudlike, to meet the pink wall.*

Every hue has its associated pastel, which means that there are at least as many possible pastel colors as there are hues—and the range of available pastels has never been as varied as it is today. While rose, sky blue, and daffodil yellow are traditional nursery pastels, the contemporary baby is being exposed to peach, apricot, apple green, mint, pale aqua, ice blue, and lavender, often in harmony. Nostalgic grayed and dusty shades and naive chalky shades are also finding their way into the nursery.

Neoclassical architects associated with postmodernism, such as Michael Graves, have made exquisite use of these more unusual pastels, which lend an air of lightness and repose to their designs while not compromising the sophistication and elegance inherent to their style. At the same time recent trends in California style have shown a fresh, fun use of the more saturated pastels.

The recent revival of old techniques for surface treatments also has important implications for the use of pastels. Walls or furnishings that are sponged, glazed, or washed with color often achieve a modulated, dappled, and luminous effect from the fact that the pigment is very diluted so that the white undercoat shows through—just as the white of a Canson paper shows through under the artist's pastel crayon. Tints may be applied directly to wet whitewashed plaster, or rubbed into white-painted or bleached wood. Often with such treatments the clear, watery feeling of the tint is very evocative.

▲ *A geometric symphony of updated pastels—brighter and more subtly defined than their traditional counterparts—is thrown into relief by the bright red of large alphabet letters below the painted wood trim, above. In contrast to the warm wall tones, the cool, pale blue ceiling seems to rise up, skylike, toward infinity.*

◀ *Natural wood is complemented by a combination of unusual pastels, hand-painted and stenciled on the wall of a small nursery, left. The luminosity and softened edges of the background colors were achieved through special paint techniques, including sponging.*

BRIGHTS

We tend to think of primaries as kid colors, not baby colors, remembering first crayons, stacking blocks, balloons, and other trappings of early childhood. The first words children learn tend to be the names of things most important to them, and among those names one usually finds *red, yellow,* and *blue.* But the child's attraction to primaries begins at birth. The first color a baby focuses on and a favorite of the first months is red. Primaries are essential, fully saturated hues—pure sensations at their most intense.

Primaries speak a bright, clear, and utterly simple language. They are unmixed and so contain no tensions. They are the most stable of colors. Green and orange, since they are mixed in evenly balanced proportions, share these qualities to a large extent, and are for practical purposes referred to as primaries. Together these elemental colors constitute a universal language. They have been the mainstays of folk art and decoration throughout the world, endowed through much of history with magical properties. They are universally symbolic, representing fundamental,

▲ *Primary-colored pencils are kids' stuff, making this pencil-legged table and stools set, above, a fun addition to the nursery art area. The paint-spattered horse is an invitation both to ride, and to paint.*

◄ *On the children's mezzanine of a loft apartment, a bold color scheme is introduced by an oversized, inflatable crayon suspended from the ceiling, left. Many simple and functional children's furnishings and accessories, such as these foam-constructed, flip armchairs, are produced in bright primary colors that fit in perfectly with a child's toys.*

▲ *Primary-colored crib bumpers lend a clean, bright look to the nursery, above. Wallpaper, wall hangings, painted trim, and rug combine to make a unified color scheme based on primaries.*

▲ *Rich primary colors—dynamic yellows, reds, and blues—decorate the canvas chairs, charming toy soldiers, and patterned wallpaper of this nursery, above.*

abstract qualities and primal feelings. A pure red, for instance, the sensation of which actually quickens the heartbeat and warms the body, symbolizes passion, aggression, sometimes danger. Red is powerful enough to scare away evil spirits, making it traditionally a lucky color. Chinese baby carriers are red for just this reason.

"Pure color is a fundamental raw material, as indispensable to life as water and fire," wrote Fernand Léger, one of the leaders of post-cubist art in Paris. In Germany during the 1920s artists, architects, and designers at the Bauhaus were developing the aesthetic of modernism, based on essential shapes and essential, or primary, colors. The modernist aesthetic in home design has almost become a part of history, yet the Bauhaus cradle, with its flat planes of red, yellow, and blue, is being produced again today, and the fresh, playful look of simple primary-colored shapes and forms still lives in all manner of things made for children—from "high tech" tubular metal nursery furnishings, to shiny wooden learning toys, to primary plastic storage bins.

This has become the primary color style of the city, with its traffic signs, taxicabs, and enameled signs. With a background of clean, white walls, it depends on the strong contrasts offered by bold primaries, which, being unmixed, always stand apart from each other. In textiles this style is epitomized by modern Scandinavian design. The nursery fabrics and wall coverings produced by Marimekko, for instance, use playful, primary shapes against white, achieving the crisp, clean feel that conjures up brightly clothed skiers on snowy slopes. These designs, whether they are composed of abstract shapes or emblematic rabbits, cars, or helicopters, show that the use of primaries in the nursery can be both fun and gently stimulating.

◄ *A bunch of cloth balloons provides wonderful rounded shapes, primary color, and softness to a nursery wall, left.*

There are other primary styles that, while bold, are warm and relaxed as well. The lyrical use of primaries in Eastern European folk art, with its exuberantly hand-painted wooden furniture, is being revived today by artists and craftsmen producing for children, as are the stenciling and quilting traditions that put primary colors into dark early American rooms. The tropical primaries of Latin America, woven together with turquoise and magenta, are finding expression in the nursery through painted tin toys, Mexican painted tin wall pieces, and bright, stripy, vegetable-dyed rugs. And there are the nursery fantasy styles—bright-painted rustic woodwork and gingerbread trim inspired by Hansel and Gretel; bold circus stripes, circus wagon toy chests, big top ceilings; and the rich, warm primary compositions of children's book illustration, particularly from the forties and fifties. A classic example is the nursery that flows through the pages of Margaret Wise Brown's gentle story *Goodnight Moon*. Though obviously vast, this "great green room" has been a comfort to little children since 1947, with its intimate green walls and deep red carpet, its tall, red-framed window half hidden behind a drape of green and yellow stripes, its blue and yellow accents, all lit by warm golden lamplight while the deep blue sky outside twinkles with stars.

Primaries used as accents of color in toys, furnishings, or fabrics serve as bright keynotes in the nursery. But when large surfaces like walls, ceilings, and floors are painted or covered in primary colors, the entire nursery becomes an environmental experience. Explaining the expanse of blue wall in his painting *Portrait of an Artist Friend*, Vincent van Gogh told his brother, "I paint infinity, a simple background of the richest, most intense blue that I can contrive." Van Gogh's blue wall, his yellow bedroom in the "yellow house" paintings, the flat, saturated interiors of Matisse in paintings like *Red Studio*, show that when a wall becomes a field of color, it becomes an expanse of pure sensation. Unconnected with any particular object, the experience of a wall entirely filled with primary hue is a reflection of the direct way in which babies and children respond to color.

Today, primary-colored walls have become softer, rich and painterly. Gone are the hard, graphic effects that were the legacy of the sixties' fascination with comic book and poster art. Hues now tend to be flat and slightly powdery, like children's tempera paints. Color may fade toward the corners or its edges may be ragged. Surfaces may be chalky, scratched, or dry and brushy. Pure pigment may be rubbed directly into plaster, creating a rich, textural color effect. As many walls of the past demonstrate so clearly, the use of primary colors on large areas is not a cut-and-dry stylistic choice.

▲ *Pure colors, like pure shapes, have an immediate impact, and their names are among a child's first words, above. This poster emphasizes learning the names of shapes even as it picks up on the room's primary colors.*

◄ *Cheerful yellow, accented in a bunch of tulips, is just one of the many bright colors that look as if they have been crayoned by a child's hand onto the papered wall, left.*

PATTERN

The language of color is incomplete without pattern. If color can be said to represent the primal element in human experience and the urge to communicate, pattern represents human evolution and the urge to design. The first culture to consciously create visual pattern for its own sake was that of ancient Egypt, which, blessed with the fertile soil of the Nile Valley, had the time to sit back and contemplate the meaning of life. The Egyptians, who four thousand years ago created pattern and with it the concept of ornamentalism, also invented the calendar to mark the passage of time.

Pattern is rhythm. The rhythm of breath; the rhythm of night and day; the rhythm of a rocking cradle or of a child's swing; the rhythm of stripes of light filtered through venetian blinds; the rhythm of squares in a garden trellis—these are all patterns, because they are repetitive.

Pattern is order. Since pattern is inherent in nature, we speak of nature as a design; where there is no pattern, we speak of randomness or chaos. Pattern is also movement—fast, slow, sweeping, or lilting. The graceful sweep of the arabesque in dance is named after a sweeping motif used in arabic patterns. And, like the division of cells that produces life, pattern is growth.

Expert theories are divided on the origins of man-made pattern. Many believe that pattern originated in the home industries of the Minoan civilization of ancient Crete, where sea-inspired motifs began to appear in the weaving of rush mats, the stitching of animal skins, and the trial and error process of making pots. Others believe that pattern began as the ritual repetition of fundamental symbolic shapes. Zigzags, circles and squares, spirals, sunbursts were the basis for primitive pattern, and because of their powerful universal appeal they are still with us today. They are also often the first shapes attempted by the unpracticed hand of the child.

Pattern is the abstraction of nature through geometry; all the shapes of traditional pattern are derived from nature. In ancient Egypt, the human hand guided by the

▲ *The openness of this patterned paper, above, with its gently twisting and intertwining sprigs against a cool, lavender ground, makes it suitable for covering an entire room without risking an oppressive feeling. Expanses of white-painted woodwork and white drapes relieve the pattern.*

▶ *A frieze on the wainscot portion of wallpaper from a child's room, right, combines simple images (sailboat, stripes, dots, zigzags) to create a graphic, sophisticated, and pleasing pattern.*

◀ *Three delicate and orderly patterns are effectively combined in this nursery, left. Window shades in a Victorian cottage-style print of small, ribbon-tied posies framed by pink ribbons coordinate perfectly with the wallpaper's tiny pink dots and integrated floral border. The linear pattern of the border's scalloped edges lends a stability to the room's composition.*

▼ *A beautiful log cabin patterned quilt, below, demonstrates the abstract "op-art" quality of many traditional folk art designs. The unevenness of the piecing and the variety of fabric prints give this type of pattern an accessibility and warmth that make it suitable for the nursery.*

mind began to simplify those shapes and to put them into decorative order. With the spread of Islam, while astronomers observing the desert stars laid the foundations for modern mathematics, pattern evolved into a highly developed and intricate art form, a product of the intellect.

The evolution of pattern is almost a reflection of individual development from birth. Babies are incapable of making pattern, yet they are fascinated by it. Whether it is the play of light through summer trees or the abstracted flowers evenly scattered on a mother's dress, the infant seems to need the focus for contemplation that patterns provide, just as much as the sensory experience of color. Recognition of pattern is a baby's first intellectual exercise; probably it is the infant's way of finding order in the chaos of new and strange sensations. This makes easily understood, regular patterns not only challenging to babies, but comforting to them as well.

There are many explanations, but no definitive answer, for the strong attraction felt by babies and children to pattern, much as the rhythmic rocking of a lullaby soothes the newborn in ways that are only half understood. But we do know from recent studies that small babies seem to prefer geometric patterns and are especially attracted by boldly patterned contrasts between black and white or bright colors of contrasting values. It is also clear that in the first months the baby is, as childcare specialist Penelope Leach writes in *Baby and Child: From Birth to Age Five* (1977), "programmed to give his attention to complex patterns and shapes because he must learn a complex visual world."

When the nursery is a rich, yet clearly stated visual environment, children quickly learn to read their complex visual world. Emblematic blue bunnies or yellow abstracted house shapes soon become identifiable, and before long the toddler takes a crayon and attempts to draw a pattern; first a circle, then a repeat of circles, following the course of primitive man. The most growable nursery patterns manage to combine a simple allover element that is immediately attractive to babies with a more complex, possibly narrative element that will hold the attention of a child. Walter Crane's Sleeping Beauty wallpaper of 1879 is a fine example of decorative storytelling, with its allover pattern of gently swirling brambles among which lie the sleeping figures of the spellbound court.

Passed down through generations, transplanted from continent to continent, patterns have evolved, never losing their original magnetism. Painted, cut, woven, printed, hammered, twisted, scratched, tiled, and stamped, the themes and motifs have remained constant. William Morris, one of the most inventive decorative artists of his time, borrowed the elements of his patterns from traditional models. The paisley pattern, a popular pattern for men's clothing and boy babies' nurseries, was derived from a certain leaf in Persian textiles that was inspired by the wind-tipped cyprus tree. It originated on Indian shawls, traveled to France and Scotland in the late nineteenth century, and made its way to the New World updated, redefined, and now gracing nursery borders and chairs instead of clothing—but still recognizably paisley. Just as fairy tales and nursery rhymes have been adapted and repeated by children over the centuries, so pattern in the nursery has been kept alive. Not much has changed besides colors, combinations, and rhythms, in tune with the changes of history.

A warm and comfortable looking child's room, left, has been created through a seemingly random meeting of diverse patterns. Yet the mix is far from haphazard. The rectilinear zigzagging of the carpet's woven pattern is reflected in the open diamonds on the bedspread, whose scattering of flowers is echoed in scattered bows and flowers on the pillowcases, and in hand-stenciled pinwheels on the table and chairs set. A hand-stenciled pinwheel frieze introduces a lighthearted tone, and leads the eye gently around the room. The openness and regularity of the frieze contrast with the effect of the dense, stippled pattern on the walls.

Today, borrowings are often eclectic, combining pattern elements from different cultures or periods. Blue and white pinstripes have been borrowed for little boys' crib sheets, edged with eyelet. The little red house that appears on Early American quilts has become a frieze stenciled on a nursery wall. A nursery dado is filled with freehand, pastel harlequin diamonds, while the floor is bordered with a hand-painted checkerboard pattern inspired by art-deco tiling. Designers are also unearthing a host of historical patterns from various eras forgotten during the spare years of modernism.

Borrowings may be from pictures in books, especially from nineteenth-century examples, the golden age of children's book illustration. There is a precedent for this: illustrations from the works of Kate Greenaway, for instance, were reproduced and put into repeat on nursery wallpapers of the period. Delicate, light, and narrative in the simplest way, these and other late Victorian papers by children's illustrators were the nursery's answer to William Morris's dark, dense acanthus leaves in the living room. The simple monochromatic woodcuts from eighteenth-century chapbooks and toy books, reproduced on custom-made rubber stamps and stamped directly onto walls, have also been used as a source of nursery pattern.

Other sources providing inspiration for the use of pattern in the nursery include Blanche Fisher Wright's illustrations for the classic *The Real Mother Goose*, first published in 1916. The images of interiors throughout the book show what can be done with pattern-on-pattern in a whimsical nursery. Tiny dotted yellow patterns in sheets tumble over simple rosebud bed skirts, while a larger rosebud print in yellow hangs as drapes. A glance through the pages provides countless indications for the use of multiple patterns. Large and small, dense and open, blue and pink, florals and gentle geometrics combine to create a pretty, textural nursery.

Janet Waring's 1937 book on Early American stencil patterns tells of an eighty-year-old woman who, on returning to visit her first home, remarked that the sight of the decorated walls there "awakened poignant memories recalling the days of her childhood, when the Chelsea china was set out with flowered teacups against the soft raspberry walls with their deep green and red decorations." Many

adults today remember vividly the patterns on their own nursery shades or bedding, and may remember the apparently common childhood habit of counting motifs, or the wonder of watching the patterns on curtains shift and change as the breeze moved them. Bold or subtle, contemporary or traditional, pattern in the nursery can be lively and decorative. But pattern in the nursery also provides a place for young eyes to rest awhile, giving the child time to ponder the curiousness of life.

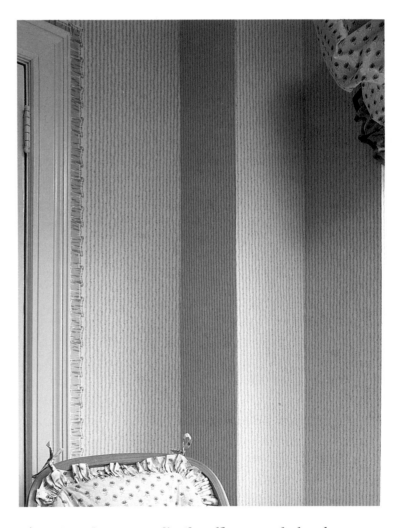

▲ *A pink, trompe l'oeil ruffle around the door meets wavy pink and white striped wallpaper, while tiny blue flowers on white adorn the ruffled chair cushion and flounced window shade in a more subdued version of the traditional pink and blue nursery, above.*

▲ *Tightly packed rows of tiny sheep, ducks, and other barnyard characters in the wallpaper, above, might look like an abstract design from a distance. But to a baby in the crib they are friends waiting for the day he learns to count them. And until that day comes, the larger animals parading around the paper frieze provide an opportunity for naming practice.*

LEARNING FROM ALICE:

PROPER PROPORTIONS

3

▲ *A tableau of a tiny wall cabinet stocked with neatly folded linens and a pair of chairs gives an Alice in Wonderland scale to the top of this chest of drawers, above.*

"Drink Me," said the label on the bottle. Being an adventurous child, Alice drank, and everyone knows what happened next. Alice's creator, Lewis Carroll, was also a professor of mathematics, and as he sat picnicking by the banks of the River Thames with his young niece Alice Liddell and her two friends, he spun a fantastic tale that played not only with the laws of logic, but also with the magic of proportion.

When Alice shrunk in size, everything in the rabbit hole seemed huge; later, as she grew to her normal proportions in the White Rabbit's house, the house suddenly became tiny. Scale and proportion were, as Alice discovered, largely a matter of perception. And perception, she must have begun to realize—being, after all, a precocious child—was a question of relativity. When Alice was tiny, the little table loomed above her head. And what had seemed within reach became frustratingly unattainable.

Thus, Alice might have deduced, not only would a normal-sized armchair seem huge to a very small person, but that same chair would also seem large in a little room, and that same little room might seem quite spacious to a tiny child. And, taking the theory to its logical conclusions (if only grown-ups could be so logical, she thought), then a ceiling, for instance, would look higher in a small room than in a large room; and to a very small person crawling across the floor, that same high-ceilinged room would seem almost infinitely tall.

Jean Piaget, the pioneering psychologist who formulated this century's most influential theories on child development, pointed out that babies and small children are only able to experience space in relation to their own bodies, and that their impressions of space are still purely sensory. Babies experience space profoundly, and subjectively; it is a psychological, not a mathematical experience. They have no background of information to tell them that the lines they see converging toward the ceiling are not really converging; they believe what they see, and they feel

SHAPING SPACE

Proper proportion, or the balancing of elements, was long ago recognized as one of the most essential aspects of architecture and design. In the second century A.D., the Egyptian neoplatonist Plotinus wrote, "What is it that impresses you when you look at something, attracts you, captivates you and fills you with joy? We are all agreed, I may say, that it is the inter-relation of parts toward one another and towards the whole, with the added element of beauty in color, which constitutes beauty as perceived by the eye; in other words, that beauty in visible things as in everything else consists of symmetry and proportion." In classical theory the concept of ideal proportion, or perfect balance, was considered paramount. Whatever man-made, be it large or small, it was to reflect the mathematical principle of the golden rectangle, an organic proportion that was so perfect it was thought to affect the spirit in a way that only pure, aesthetic beauty can.

Pioneers of modern architecture, such as Le Corbusier, revived the classical principle of the golden rule. The proportions of buildings and their rooms, they thought, should have mathematical qualities that reflected the proportions of the human body. Decoration, moldings, color—in fact all the architectural elements that had traditionally helped to give rooms their shape—were now considered obsolete. These visual details, it was thought, could only detract from the poetic effect of rooms designed as perfectly proportioned cubes with pure, white walls. Even the normally uneven plaster surfaces of walls were now smoothed to perfection.

In recent years, the ideal of perfectly and mathematically proportioned rooms has come to be recognized as only an ideal. There is the realization that space is always something of a subjective experience, psychological rather than mathematical. Proportions suggest meanings—high, "lofty" ceilings; little, "cottage" windows—and may be shaped to become an expressive element in a room. Decorative elements, from color to texture, pattern, moldings, and furnishings have come back into play as tools for shaping space and the way it is felt, in ways that are often new interpretations on old themes.

The flat, white walls preferred by modernists are again being given perceptual depth through color, pattern, and texture. And architectural detailing—moldings, cornices, arches, alcoves—is once again shaping every room in the house, including the nursery. Sometimes the unique proportions of a room might be deliberately emphasized to give it character or exaggerate a particular feeling. At other times the existing proportions may be altered perceptually, or through the simplest structural solutions. Proportion affects us in many ways, and everything about a room, including ourselves and our memories, combines to influence our perception of it. Nowhere is this more relevant than in the nursery, because the small child's experience of space is fundamentally different from that of the adult.

Increasingly, as the home becomes a designed environment and the nursery, like the child, becomes integrated into that environment, there is an attempt to restore to the nursery a sense of proportion suited to its purpose. Today, nursery design is often a kind of Alice in Wonderland endeavor, in which laws of perception provide the magical key to restoring a proper sense of proportion to a room that has traditionally been seen as the hub of the young child's entire world.

▶ *A high ceiling and tall, elegant double windows framed by floor length drapes in this classically proportioned nursery, right, suggest a formality that is offset by a cheerfully covered, enameled iron daybed and matching fabric at the windows, and by the friendly cast of characters who line the shelves.*

THE SHRINKING OF THE NURSERY

"Oh, you foolish Alice!" says Alice midway through her fourth chapter in Wonderland, with her head almost bursting through the roof of the White Rabbit's house. "How can you learn lessons in here? Why, there's hardly room for *you*, and no room at all for any lesson-books!"

Through much of its history, the nursery was a sizeable room. Often banished from most of the rest of the house, children created entire worlds in their own rooms. The nursery or nursery suite may have served as bedroom, playroom, and schoolroom for at least one child, and for the ubiquitous nurse besides. Classic children's stories and book illustrations offer a glimpse of the proportions considered ideal in the Victorian nursery—chair rails and picture rails encircled the room, defining the edges of space; pictures, friezes, knickknacks filled the room with excitement; and separate areas were defined for various kinds of activity, for example, a little table and chairs for work or snack, a cozy nook under a dipping ceiling, perhaps a window seat or alcove for reading and dreaming.

Playrooms and playhouses especially were large-scale and many-faceted. The vast playroom that Frank Lloyd Wright, father of six children, designed at Oak Park, Illinois, must be one of the most spectacular children's rooms in this century's architectural history. With its cathedral ceiling, its minstrel's gallery and inglenook, this playroom was practically a temple, devoted to the free play of the child's imagination.

In 1849 (just fifteen years before Carroll introduced the world to Alice's struggles with proportion) the health educator William Walcott complained in his book *The Young Mother* that since it was generally the extra room in the house that was now selected for a nursery, and since extra rooms tended to be the smallest in the house, contemporary nurseries were often small and badly proportioned; not particularly suited, he reasoned, "for their purpose."

Walcott's writings heralded the modern era—not only in architecture, but also in family life, and in nursery life. Modest, servantless homes with small, efficient rooms were

▶ *This tiny nursery, right, with its steeply pitched ceiling, was made to look airy yet cozy through a careful orchestration of design elements. The low windows were effectively squared off by hanging festoon blinds far above the top of the window frame, thereby giving the room a feeling of extra height. Furnishings, from the heart-shaped, antique side table to the hand-painted rocking chair and the ornate crib, combine function and decoration. The whole room is unified by the subtly striped wall covering that covers even the ceiling, and by the dainty, alphabet frieze whose pattern is picked up in the matching crib bumper and soft crib toys.*

being built in the suburbs, as were apartments in the cities. Children of the rising middle class were slowly being integrated into the grown-up world, encroaching on adult territory. The nursery as a room was losing its importance as the child's primary domain.

Before long, babies were allowed to crawl on living room carpets, and toddlers rode tricycles through kitchens, and more than ever before the baby was crammed into that extra room in the house, the nursery having become more of a glorified bedroom than the all-purpose room it once was. Big rooms, like big station wagons, are becoming a thing of the past in family life. Rambling houses have given way to smaller homes, and families are growing in tiny city apartments. Ceilings, once high, are now economically low, and large, old rooms have been subdivided to make two or three.

Today, especially in apartments where space is at a premium, the nursery is often created where no room previously existed: in a corner of the living room or master bedroom, separated off to house a new baby; or in a child's bedroom, divided to create a newborn nursery. Not only have nursery proportions decreased drastically, but also the sense of proportion itself—the relationship between floor size and ceiling height, window dimensions, and other architectural features—has in many cases been lost.

▲ *A wall-mounted, swing-arm lamp is an attractive and efficient space-saver in the child's room, above. The door to an adjoining bathroom has been fitted with a full length mirror, which reflects light and creates a spatial illusion.*

◀ *A sense of spaciousness in this busy but uncluttered nursery, left, is achieved with the help of a simple, light color scheme and furnishings that do more than one job—a decorative Peter Rabbit coat-tree, a spaceship/rocker/chair, and a shelving unit that incorporates a changing table and creates an alcove for a cozy window seat.*

MAKING SMALL ROOMS SEEM BIGGER

Stuck in the White Rabbit's house, Alice had little recourse but to eat a tiny cake in the hope that she would shrink to fit the room (children are notoriously literal). But in the real world children grow, and their environment appears to shrink. What Alice probably didn't realize was that there are countless ways of making a room appear smaller or larger, of making ceilings seem higher or lower, of making furniture appear compact or bulky. Based on theories of perception, on how the brain interprets visual sensations, decorative visual treatments that perceptually alter space were created through much of the history of interior design, until modernist theory banned both decoration and illusionism from the home.

Perhaps the most obvious, and the most playful, example of space-expanding illusionism is trompe l'oeil. Traditionally limited to the more public areas of the home and frequently operating on the level of sophisticated wit, only now, as we begin to recognize that even small babies respond to the three-dimensional world, is trompe l'oeil finding its way into the nursery.

Reinterpreted for the nursery, the rich trompe l'oeil tradition takes on entirely new characteristics. As a device it is still expansive, because it looks three-dimensional. But it is far simpler than it ever was, both in its execution and in its imagery. Wit is being replaced by whimsy, grandeur by simplicity. Entering the world of childhood experience, designers are creating feelings of depth and fantasy to visually transform the small nursery, and in the process a new, innocent trompe l'oeil imagery is emerging.

The walls and ceiling painted to resemble puffy white clouds floating in a modulated blue sky appeal to the young child's fascination with the roof of nature, and create an airy feeling. In a highly baroque nursery designed in 1923 by Oscar Kaufman, clouds on the ceiling were made to extend down onto the wall and below the cornice in places. In another nursery, fairy-tale scenes cover closet doors. A gentle garden view, painted into a faux window frame over the crib, opens an entire imaginary world beyond the four walls of the nursery. Large, almost transparent soap bubbles, ready to burst, drift around a room, stimulating the growing child's developing curiosity concerning fantasy and reality.

One of England's leading contemporary trompe l'oeil muralists, Graham Rust has created intricate, often whimsical nursery murals based on themes from children's literature. As a concession to the height of his average client, he makes a point of concentrating detail in the lower portions of his murals. Another lesson is offered by a nursery designed in 1937 by the New York architect Pierre Dutel in which huge, bold, trompe l'oeil alphabet blocks appear to hurtle out of the wall. Although the concept is an attractive one for the nursery, the combination of scale and excessive movement creates a restless feeling that could have been avoided with a more gentle and playful scattering of blocks.

▶ *Function and space-saving efficiency in the form of built-in closets have been mysteriously disguised through the use of trompe l'oeil artistry, with the closet doors becoming an integral part of the fairy-tale scene that covers the walls of this small but visually expansive nursery, right. The chubby fairy, who cuddles a rabbit atop a wooden railing, invites the nursery's young occupant to imaginatively explore the wide, idyllic landscape that lies beyond the painted rose bower.*

One reason that design solutions in the nursery have tended to be flat and two-dimensional is that, until recently, it was thought that babies and small children were incapable of understanding three-dimensional space. But the science of visual perception has advanced radically, and in the process research has shown the extent to which even infants are capable of understanding and responding to simple, though subtle, visual clues—or visual illusions—concerning three-dimensional depth and space.

Trompe l'oeil is only one example in a huge range of options currently open for perceptually expanding space. In today's nursery, the light colors that have for some time been recognized as space-expanding when applied to walls, ceiling, and floor, are no longer limited to neutral white or cream, nor to traditional pastel pink or blue. A new range of light shades and effects, at once decorative and space-shaping, has found its way into the nursery— the flat, ice-cream colors of postmodernism; cool, light-infused pastels; the chalky shades of tinted plaster; the textural tints of faded fresco effects. A leading theorist of postmodern architecture, Charles Jencks painted his two-year-old daughter's nursery in the same variants of washed creams and turquoise that were used for the landing outside her room, so that when the door is open the landing seems to be a part of the room.

One way to make small rooms seem bigger is to have nursery furniture that functions at several levels, left. The stubby-legged chairs are low enough for children to sit and play near floor-level while the tiered dresser drawers make practical use of vertical space. The youth bed with its high back and sides doubles as a couch.

Along with the return of color, a new surge in inventive surface treatments has revived and developed old techniques, such as sponging, mottling, layering, and scratching, that turn flat walls into spatial, textural canvases. Such effects—a wash of clear pink fading to soft white at the corners, a stippled blue ceiling, a mottled room in pale pastels, a floor of bleached boards rubbed with lavender pigment—are being used in the nursery to deepen space while softening and enlivening the child's world. And, unlike the baby pastels once prescribed for children, these shades and effects are stimulating enough to hold a baby's interest through the nursery years.

Wallpapers printed with tiny patterns or motifs on a light ground also expand perceived space. Lewis Carroll, as a mathematician, may have explained it as inverse proportion; to Alice it may have come as another annoying contradiction—big patterns make rooms look smaller, small patterns make rooms look bigger. Due to a revival of interest in decorative wall coverings, wallpapers are now produced in everything from pretty Victorian florals to tiny geometric patterns.

In the small nursery, wallpaper scattered with little rosebuds or stars may cover walls and ceiling, acknowledging the airy charm of the tiny cottage nursery that has become a storybook ideal with its simple, sunny window and its wide board floor painted a fresh apple green or daffodil yellow. Many companies now offer coordinating wallpapers, friezes, and fabrics that, when used in conjunction, create the unified simplicity so important to any space-expanding decorating scheme.

Often small nurseries suffer more from oppressively low ceilings than they do from lack of floor space. Here again, color may play a structural role. Since light colors seem to recede into the distance, low ceilings painted or papered in pale shades seem higher. Blue—the coolest and therefore most distant-seeming of colors—remains a favorite color for nursery ceilings, perhaps because the small child tends to be fascinated with the sky as a kind of two-dimensional ceiling over the earth. With the addition of some billowy painted clouds or random stars, or a stick-on glow-in-the-dark constellation, a blue ceiling becomes a magical thing that draws the eye skyward. And considering the amount of time spent lying down during babyhood, the idea of a nursery ceiling that invites dreamy "sky gazing" seems perfectly appropriate for captivating interest.

A vertical emphasis also increases visual height in the room. Decorative mobiles or model planes, hung from the ceiling, add interest and draw the eye upward. High, vertical storage solutions, with upper shelves reserved for decorative or "special occasion" toys, have the same visual effect. Sometimes verticals are applied to the walls, in the form of a subtly striped wallpaper, or with floor to ceiling moldings—a variation on the horizontal chair and picture rail with which eighteenth- and nineteenth-century architects structured interior space—that create a series of panels in which to hang pictures or children's artwork.

▲ *Decorative tiles, dark for the lower half of the room and light for the upper half, make a children's bathroom a fun place to be, above. A goldfish shower head helps to make the bathroom an extension of the playroom.*

▶ *Whimsy, color, and light infuse this small but cheerful nursery, right. The shimmering, glass-brick wall, built up to adult, or cowboy, eye level, separates the boy's room from a stairway and landing, while allowing light to pass through from the lavender-framed window, and parents to check on the child with minimal disturbance.*

FUNCTION AND DECORATION:
WINDOWS, SCREENS, STORAGE, AND FURNITURE

Just as space is shaped by color, it is also defined by light. A small, dark room feels cramped and oppressive, whereas a bright, sunny little room can be warm and cozy. Windows, besides admitting light, frame views that expand the limits of the nursery into the wide world outside. Sheer gauzy drapes or lace curtains, swooping into graceful tie-backs, soften the framing and create an airy, diffused light in the room. Venetian blinds or roller shades in pale colors are often chosen for the small contemporary nursery, offering the option of shutting out ugly views while allowing light to enter.

The balance between mass and void, or wall and window, is an important element in the proportion of a room, and one that has changed from period to period and region to region, depending on climate, economics, and building techniques. For this reason, certain wall-to-window proportions can bring to mind architectural styles—from the tall, elegant window openings in high-ceilinged Queen Anne homes, to the chunky walls and tiny windows preferred in hot climates. Each style provides its own rhythm in the relation of wallspace to window.

While window views and the light that windows allow increase the sense of space in a room, windows that are large for a room make it feel smaller than it really is. Living lofts and other large spaces that have been divided into smaller rooms often suffer from an unbalanced ratio between window and wall area. To redress the balance, parts of the window are sometimes covered with delicate, light-filtering drapes and a low valance is added; or decorative balloon shades, in a fabric to match wallpaper or bedding, are hung to partially conceal the top of a tall window. Or, in nurseries with a country feel, a flower box on the sill shortens the window, as do simple cottage curtains in pretty cotton prints, with the top pair tied back and the lower pair left to hang.

Nurseries that have been created by dividing an existing room are sometimes opened up to the larger space with

▲ *A decoupage screen hides the open fireplace, above. Decorated in traditional style, with cut-and-pasted butterflies, borders, pages of sheet music, and images from* Alice in Wonderland, *the portable screen is also a useful nursery divider.*

▶ *Daylight streams through a gabled window to illuminate bears on the snug window-seat, right. The seat, which echoes the cottagelike feeling of the gabled ceiling, doubles as a storage chest for blankets and bed linens.*

internal windows that increase not only the sense of space, but light as well. With a window between themselves and the living room or parents' bedroom, babies feel less cut off from the world. And since from the youngest age children are by nature territorial, any suggestion that the nursery is more than a room is a definite asset. A little curtained window at child's eye level, perhaps with a planter beneath, turns the nursery into a house within a house; a simple porthole makes it a ship.

Sometimes the internal window is simply a hole cut in a plasterboard wall, in which case the possibilities for window shapes are endless — not only squares and rectangles but circles, triangles, and even animal or letter shapes. More often, real windows are installed that open and close, ventilate and soundproof. Investigations have confirmed what parents have long known — that children are essentially functionalists. They are both delighted and stimulated by things that work.

Tiny city nurseries have generated some of the most inventive design solutions, such as sliding shoji screen walls, inspired by traditional Japanese home design, that create a delightfully airy, diffused light and can be opened to integrate nursery life into family life. A nursery built in a corner of the living room in a small Manhattan apartment was separated from the main space by a high, facade-shaped screen wall. With its pitched roof and chimney stack, it is a postmodern reference to the archetypal house as every child draws it. Under the pitched roof the architect Fred Schwartz installed a clerestory window; at child's eye level he installed another, curtained window, and a planter overflowing with flowers. To lend a whimsical but real sense of privacy to this house within a room, the architect joined the screen wall to the room wall with a picket fence and its own latched gate.

Innovation in architectural design solutions for the small nursery has been matched by a range of furnishings as well as storage and lighting solutions that address spatial problems in new and innovative ways. In the past few years, manufacturers have begun to produce dual-purpose furnishings in styles ranging from colonial to high tech. Cribs of every kind are being designed with built-in storage units and night tables; some of these convert into youth or twin beds, making them both space and budget saving. A crib that turns into an adult love seat, dressers that convert into changing tables, and toy chests that double as benches are also being produced, often in styles to match one another. Custom solutions are also proliferating. One designer faced with the challenge of a tiny nursery for two little girls created a hinged wooden flap that can be lowered over the two end-to-end twin beds to make a daytime surface for games or art activities.

Storage solutions that combine function and decoration are also considered dual-purpose in small nurseries, where shortage of wall and floor space severely limits decoration-for-the-sake-of-it. Storage units shaped as palm trees or houses, toy chests designed as circus wagons, even standard units with existing handles or pulls replaced by bright colored or patterned hardware are being used to dress up the small nursery. Since little children tend to hoard, storage solutions that encourage orderly tidiness help to keep small nurseries uncluttered. The options are varied and adaptable — wicker baskets or plastic storage bins in various sizes and colors that can be stacked on open shelving; rolling carts holding art or construction materials; bright-colored "fishing" nets that can be hung above a crib or bed and piled high with stuffed animals and dolls. Decorative lighting solutions are also space-saving. Floor lamps designed like huge, glowing crayons, and whimsical nursery sconces leave precious table surfaces free. Some of these lamps can be dimmed to double as night-lights.

▶ *Sometimes nursery life spills out into the hallway. To allow the child expanding space, the design theme of the nursery has been continued in the area outside the nursery doors, right, complete with grassy carpet and sunny-colored shelving. The child-sized bear chair invites a browse through the shelf library.*

The simple, tidy little nursery has a charm all of its own. This is the one room in the house that can be designed to suggest a scale proportionate to the child, making a delightful, doll's house environment that feels safe and comfortable during those first subjective years. The scaled-down nursery approach is naturally space-saving, but as one of the most charming of nursery traditions, it is an equally viable approach for the larger room.

Alice Liddell's own childhood nursery was probably furnished with scaled-down replicas of the grown-up pieces that graced the rest of the house: one or two small upholstered armchairs, and perhaps a sofa, just like those in the parlor; a child-sized table and chairs where she could do her schoolwork, play her games, and eat her toast and jam; a tiny rocking chair for book browsing; maybe even a tiny piano. Scaled-down children's furniture has been made through much of the history of furniture itself; perhaps it originated with the idea, prevalent until the 1800s, that children were essentially miniature adults. In the record books of a seventeenth-century stenciler we find references to a child's "Round Post Bannister," and a child's Boston rocker whose small headpiece was to be stenciled with the letters of the alphabet.

Today, proper scale and proportion in the nursery is possible with a choice of new, antique, or used pieces. Sturdy child-sized upholstered chairs and sofas are being found in yard sales and reupholstered to match or contrast with drapes or bedding. Antique children's rockers and wicker furnishings are available, and new pieces are also being produced in a wide variety of styles ranging from elegant Queen Anne or streamlined fifties, to reinterpreted folk or Conran modern. These include armchairs, table and chair sets, daybeds, sofas, love seats, screens — even fun, spongy, dinosaur- or bear-shaped chairs whose "arms" wrap around the child. Many of the upholstered pieces are now constructed of foam. Light enough to be carried by very small people who like to rearrange their rooms for visitors or dolls' tea parties, some of these even open up into a small bed for occasional sleep-overs — a definite asset in the small nursery.

Architectural design elements are also being used to create a scaled-down nursery feel. Extra-low chair rails encircle rooms large and small, providing a close-to-the-ground zone that can define the small child's private world. Since their function is primarily visual, these rails are sometimes faked with painted lines, stenciled patterns, or narrow, printed borders. In traditional nurseries, reproduction wood trim is often used, while in the contemporary nursery a chunky, squared-off or half-round wooden rail, reminiscent of toddler building blocks, acknowledges the small child's response to simple, tactile stimulation. Scaled-down means low, but not necessarily small. For instance, door knobs and drawer pulls at child's height are often chosen for large-scale graspability. By playing with scale, designers are creating Alice in Wonderland rooms in response to the way children view the world.

◄ *In order to make this high-ceilinged room, left, more manageable for a small child, the design emphasis has been concentrated in the lower part of the room, creating a child-height zone conducive to play, sleep, and work. Long, low windows help to define this close-to-the-ground space, while a soffit creates a protectively low ceiling over the sleeping area. Built-in shelf and cubbies around the bed for bedtime storybooks and nighttime friends, and a giant crayon night-light make this area cozily self-contained. A low but spacious desk and sofa further emphasize the child's viewpoint, and a soft, pink carpet makes floor-play both warm and comfortable.*

MAKING LARGE ROOMS COZY

Had Alice not almost drowned in a pool of her own tears, it might be easy to forget that some nurseries suffer from a feeling of too much space, especially when the occupant is very tiny. If the nursery is to be a safe refuge from the world of "High bare walls, great bare floor . . . Great big people perched on chairs," as Robert Louis Stevenson remembered the world of adults in *A Child's Garden of Verses*, then it must be comfortingly cozy without feeling cramped. Of course, as babies grow into children and begin to accumulate large-scale toys like train sets and play kitchens, a spacious nursery becomes a real asset. But as in the too-small nursery, proportions can be altered perceptually, if not structurally, through the use of color, pattern, and architectural detailing.

Just as pale colors appear to recede, thereby expanding space, darker colors give the illusion of shrinking space. Although the nursery is generally associated with light rather than dark tones, the need to cozy up a large room has provided the perfect opportunity for some bold and unusual color schemes. Walls and woodwork in playful primaries, softened with colorful hangings and plenty of cheerful fabric on beds and windows; hot, Mexican colors set off with shutter green wicker furnishings and window shades, and crisp white bedding; a navy blue wall as a backdrop for brightly colored toys or brightly painted folk art furniture. Darker wall colors also invite the application of stenciling, either in traditional or contemporary patterns. Together, color and detailing can help to separate areas within the nursery, creating a varied and stimulating visual environment.

Here, too, is an opportunity to let loose all the wonderful patterns and narratives that exist in wallpapers, friezes, nursery fabrics, and bedding. Whereas in the small nursery some sense of unity is all-important if a cluttered feeling is to be avoided, in the large nursery almost anything goes. The larger the pattern, the more it tends to shrink the space. One designer created a flamboyant fairground nursery for two preschool boys, in which all four walls are papered with a carousel animal print and the ceiling is lowered with an actual big top made of circus-striped fabric.

Other examples of cozy, large nursery solutions include custom-made bed canopies that keep the monsters at bay, or even a four-poster crib produced by at least one manufacturer. The noted child psychologist Bruno Bettelheim once wrote that children equate sky with mother, both being protective and enclosing. For, as Bettelheim wrote, "life on a small planet surrounded by limitless space seems awfully lonely and cold to a child." The nursery ceiling, or false ceiling, can serve the same reassuring function for a child as the sky.

Often a sprawling room lacks intimacy mainly because it lacks definition. A room whose edges are defined feels more comfortable; there is a sense of order, and for small children, order can bring comfort and security. The need to define space in the large nursery invites the introduction of moldings and trim. Like the horizon line, horizontal bands of color are restful to the eye. Chair rails, picture rails, and wainscoting, painted in colors complementary to the overall scheme, are used to lend serenity to the large nursery while defining the limits of space. Friezes and borders break up large expanses of wall; placed below a picture rail they also perceptually lower ceiling height.

▶ *Inside a room-within-a-room, right, a carpeted bench and useful shelves under a child-height ceiling create the coziest of nooks for reading, daydreaming, or joining a pretend birthday party. The entire playhouse/bed is shown on the following page.*

Faced with the task of designing a room for his two children, New York architect Ari Bahat decided to look at the space from their close-to-the-ground viewpoint. Kneeling on the floor, he discovered that although the space did not appear to expand much, the nine-foot ceiling seemed to double in height. This realization led him to divide the nursery space vertically, instead of horizontally, by creating a railed, loft playhouse/spaceship/guest area that hung low in the center of the room.

With the recent blossoming of design for children, and the revival of artisanship, there is practically no end to the possibilities for cozying up the large nursery. Whether decorative elements are chosen from among the huge range of options in coordinated nursery wall coverings, borders, friezes, and fabrics, or are commissioned from stencilers, mural painters, custom printers, and weavers, spatial solutions today are possible in every style, including the most personal and eclectic.

◀ *An innovative approach to making a large nursery both comfortable and fun for a small child, left, relies on a multipurpose playhouse/bed to break up the space into kid-sized areas. The roof of the "cottage" is cut away between the gables, making a cozy sleeping area accessible by the stairway, which incorporates under-the-stairs storage drawers. The picket fence, on rolling casters, serves as a movable toy bin.*

▲ *A custom-made bed canopy, comprised of a length of sparsely printed, light diffusing fabric loosely stretched over a pair of suspended wooden dowels and draped to the floor, effectively creates false walls and ceiling for a cozy sleeping area, above.*

◀ *On the other side of the canopied sleeping area is a small and welcoming corner for art, games, and entertainment, left.*

WHO'S BEEN SITTING IN MY CHAIR?

IDENTITY, GENDER, AND NUMBER

▲ *A sturdy, heirloom toy cupboard, above, is filled with the treasured possessions that reveal much of a child's identity.*

Nobody knows where Goldilocks came from, or where she disappeared to after escaping through the window of the three bears' house. But few would disagree with Bruno Bettelheim, who sees the story of "Goldilocks and the Three Bears" as an allegory about privacy, possession, and territory within the family circle. Goldilocks, says Bettelheim in *The Uses of Enchantment* (1977), is a little girl in search of her personal identity. The bear family, with its three bowls, three chairs, and three beds, represents the human family in which father, mother, and baby are each comfortably sure of their roles and identities — until the intruding Goldilocks arrives.

"Who's been sitting in MY chair?" booms Father Bear on seeing that his personal territory has been invaded. The territorial instincts of animals are well known. With the aid of secretions, roars, and bristling fur, animals appropriate space and mark territories within which they can safely feed, mate, and rear their young. Humans are instinctually territorial too. On the simplest level, a teenager arriving in summer camp pins a favorite poster and photo of a friend to the wall next to her assigned bunk bed, and calls it home. Personal space regulates privacy, helps our sense of identity, and gives order to our lives.

Home, and all of its parts, is the human's primary territory. Defined on the outside by walls, doors, hedges, and Keep Out signs, and on the inside by particular colors, patterns, ornamentation, objects, and furnishings, the home allows us to be who we are and to develop our sense of self. But the human family, like the bear family in the folk tale, is made up of separate individuals with different tastes, preferences, and needs dependent on age, gender, and personality. Even twins need the opportunity to develop separate personalities, different senses of self. In cultures such as ours, where individualism is valued above the common will and *identity crisis* has become a commonplace phrase, and where even small babies have finally been recognized as personalities in their own right, the problem of creating individualized nursery spaces has become both an imperative and a major challenge. The challenge is amplified when space is tight and children have to share rooms.

In our overcrowded, overly homogeneous world, with our mass-produced housing, fixtures, and furnishings, it is personal style that enables us to differentiate ourselves from our neighbors and to create a world that is identifiably ours, in a room that may be essentially identical to fifty others in the same apartment building or housing complex. "Personalizing is the human way of adapting to environments," says Joan Kron in her book *Home-Psych: The Social Psychology of Home and Decoration* (1983).

It is the personalizing of space—the social scientist's term for decorating—that helps to define identity; on the other hand, the existence of separate rooms, dependent on the floor plan of the house rather than on any decorating scheme, is what makes privacy possible. Usually plan and decorating scheme work together. But sometimes, for instance when two children share a room, decorating schemes must do the work of both. The more subtly individualized these schemes are, the more effectively they do their job. Giving a brother and sister separate areas defines ownership and limits bickering; giving those separate areas personal decorating touches helps each child define his or her identity, and respect the space of the other.

"Someone's been eating from my bowl," says a horrified Mother Bear. Small children sympathize with this tale of invasion because they themselves are experiencing the most territorial of all life stages. Toddlers are famous for their inability to share possessions, a tendency that child development experts see not as a lack of generosity, but as a sign that babies equate material things, including their chairs, beds, and rooms, with their own brand new sense of self. Soon after a baby begins to move independently, creeping or crawling away from the safety of adults into the great unknown, he or she is suddenly faced with a sense of separateness, which poses a brand new problem—"Who am I?" Like Goldilocks, the small child is in search of his or her identity, and to a large extent a personalized nursery environment can help him or her to establish that separate selfhood.

▲ *Rockers painted in Pennsylvania Dutch–style motifs, hats holding dried flowers, and special pillows on bed and chair give this girl's room, above, a sweet "old-fashioned" style.*

▲ *Handmade quilts, above, make wonderful heirlooms for a child to grow up with on his or her bed or wall, and eventually to pass on to the next generation when the child becomes an adult.*

Finding a personal slant to nursery decoration can be one of the most rewarding aspects in the creation of a child's room, whether the child is little more than a name and a due date, or a tiny newborn, or a toddler with his or her own color preferences and favorite story characters. Perhaps this accounts for the fact that the nursery is the one room in the house that is seldom given over altogether to the interior designer or decorator; it is the room into which the family tends to have the most input. When it comes to nursery design, it is the parents who define the identity of the baby, tending to give full reign to their own version of an ideal childhood.

Before the days of mass consumption, homes and the nurseries they housed evoked the individual identities of the families who lived in them by virtue of craftsmanship and artisanship. In eighteenth- and early nineteenth-century America, when journeyman artists traveled from village to village and from home to home, the whole family would gather to choose background colors, motifs, and borders from the artist's kit. Although the same kit of color and stencil was offered to each family, the results could vary widely. The individuality of stenciled walls resulted from the various combinations of small motifs. Often motifs were chosen for sentimental, personal, or symbolic reasons. Hearts and bells spoke of joy and happiness; the sunburst, the wave motif, and the heart have, from the time of the Assyrians, symbolized creation and fertility, and may therefore have been picked by eighteenth-century parents to represent a birth in the family.

Today, artists are once again coming into the home, bringing their paints and brushes, their stencils and their sketches. With the recent revival of artisanship—not only muralists, stencilers, and special effects painters, but also furniture-makers and -painters, custom rug loomers, and so on—the possibilities for individualizing the nursery have become wide-ranging and exciting. Many artists and craftspeople now specialize in nursery decor, and small companies offering custom services to clients can reproduce or adapt anything from color swatches to wallpaper designs, book illustrations, sketches, or photographs. A motif on a special pillowcase has been copied onto a nursery rug and closet door; a child's first drawing has been made into a rubber stamp and used to create wall pattern. In a sense, the nursery is stepping back into the past of individualized decoration, yet the results are often far from traditional.

Stenciling, with its naive charm, has been revived as a popular means of personalizing the nursery. It may take the form of a rediscovered, eighteenth-century stencil design, or a new, hand-cut stencil decoration featuring anything from gingerbread men to stars and moons. A preschool child might make his or her own special request—a frieze of baseball bats or ribbons and bows. The same stencil may be repeated on walls, floor, a toy chest, even bed linens and furnishing fabrics.

Family tradition represents an important aspect of the child's sense of self. Heirloom cradles, grandfather's pull-toys, decoratively framed family portraits help the small child to place him or herself within a personally meaningful history. Favorite storybook themes remembered from the parents' own childhood often provide material for motifs that can be stenciled, painted freehand, or even rubber-stamped onto cribs, chests, and walls as murals or friezes. And since such classic characters as Peter Rabbit, Squirrel Nutkin, and Babar have found their way onto everything from nursery lamps to musical boxes and wall clocks, it is possible to create an entire storybook theme nursery that conjures up a timeless fantasy world populated by beloved friends of childhoods past and present.

There is a popular children's chant, repeated for generations, that centers on whatever is the first letter of the child's name: "B my name is Brian, my favorite color is Blue and I like Buses." Even before they can verbalize, babies feel themselves to be inseparable from their names; the self and the name, or a little later the initial, are one and the same thing. It is perhaps for this reason that a baby's name or initial often provides the clue for individualized nursery decoration.

Names are painted onto toy chests, chair headboards, bed headboards, closets, even walls. One New York muralist makes a specialty of intricately lettered wall decoration that makes of the child's name both a verbal and an attractive visual entity. In the design of his own daughter Lily's nursery, the notable architectural historian Charles Jencks developed a stylized lily motif that he used both as a stencil on the wardrobe and door, and as a cutout shape

▲ *Three-dimensional alphabet letters, above, are a fun and decorative way of personalizing the child's room.*

▲ *A girl's bed dressed in white ruffles, satin, and lace, above, characterizes an idealized notion of femininity.*

for drawer handholes. An almost geometrical abstraction of the water lily, this stylization and its delicate use in the room is reminiscent of the rose motif that became an integral part of nearly every room created by turn-of-the-century Scottish architect Charles Rennie Mackintosh, including the folk-inspired playroom for his unrealized project "House for an Art Lover," designed for a major architectural competition.

Once, some part of the identity of a child's home would have been provided by the environment immediately surrounding it, whether by flowers from the garden, building materials and even pigments from the surrounding land, or rugs woven from locally produced yarns. Today, the small world that is the child's immediate environment is once again, but in quite different ways, providing a variety of sources for nursery motifs.

Leaves found on neighborhood outings have been used to create stencil patterns for a nursery floor. The mother of one baby had the nursery rug custom-loomed to incorporate a picture of the facade of the family's house. In another nursery sits a dollhouse that is a perfect scale model of the child's home, including her own room, complete with wall coverings and furnishings. And a furniture-maker was commissioned to produce a low folding screen, intended to separate a nursery play area, that was painted with a detailed representation of the street on which the child's house stood.

Making fundamental decorating choices for a baby who is newborn or yet to be born is almost like choosing the baby's name before he can say who he is, and the same kinds of factors come into play in both decisions: family tradition, a personal favorite, something appealing found in the pages of a book, something that harmonizes with other family rooms or with the overall style of the house. Just as babies are sometimes named after their month of birth, so nursery color schemes have been based on the color of the baby's birthstone, and astrological birth symbols have been stenciled onto cradles. But the most decisive factor in both naming a baby and decorating the newborn nursery is generally the baby's gender.

PUPPY DOGS' TAILS: FOR A BOY

The first thing any parent knows about a new baby is whether the tiny wriggling thing is made of sugar and spice and all things nice, or of snaps and snails and puppy-dogs' tails—in other words, the baby's sexual identity. This is also one of the first ways in which the baby will define him or herself. Many years have passed since Dr. Spock first advised parents against the reinforcement of sexual stereotypes in babies and young children. Yet, whether traditional boy or girl preferences for certain colors and motifs are innate or culturally imposed, it seems that most children by the age of three or so have placed themselves firmly, if temporarily, on the side of either pinks and lavenders and frills and flowers, or bold blues and reds, trains and trucks. Sexual identity is the young child's way of relating to the world, and some parents choose to accentuate this tendency.

"You cannot decorate a room before you know its gender," writes Joan Kron in *Home-Psych* (1983). The newborn nursery is traditionally feminine in gender. It is softly colored, pretty, delicate in texture, whether it is baby blue or baby pink, for a boy or for a girl. Perhaps this is a legacy of early Victorian days, when infants of both sexes were clothed in dresses and small boys as well as girls were given dolls to play with; days in which babies, male and female, were considered frail and delicate creatures. Bright colors, it was thought in Victorian times, could injure the eyes of little children.

The tradition of the feminine newborn nursery still lives today, making it a challenge to find a color that will still work for a baby boy when the baby is three and overtly boyish. Sometimes, softening techniques such as sponging, mottling, or stenciling are used to take the bite out of walls painted in the bolder or darker "boy" colors. Other boy nursery solutions defy tradition, acknowledging that babies of both genders are robust enough to withstand, and even enjoy bolder color schemes.

One baby boy's nursery was painted a navy blue and accented with white trim, creating a backdrop that emphasized the vivid primaries of the boy's toys and of the brightly hand-painted, folk-style furnishings. Another contrasts a bright enamel red "baby block" crib and simple, primary-painted storage against mottled, castle gray walls. The bright pastels of California style have also been used as fun, growable baby boys' colors, sometimes in conjunction with bold geometrics such as tiled or painted black and white checkerboard floors. Colorful stripes, checks, and plaids, eminently growable boy patterns, are visually stimulating for any baby.

▶ *In this spacious loft, right, the boys sleep above the living/play area. A parade of stuffed animals lines the ledge traversing the upper area, while on the green tabletop below, a train set and vehicles are ready for action.*

Clues for the use of textiles in the baby boy's nursery are provided by some of the infant bedding being designed for boys today, which often reconciles the soft and pretty with the masculine by combining textiles normally associated with men's fashions, and trims or appliqués that evoke the delicacy of newborn babyhood. Cotton ticking, flannel plaids, oxford stripes, updated paisleys, and chambray are softened with eyelet trim, ruffles, bows, pastel pipings, and lamb motifs.

Color and pattern identity is only one factor in the sexual identity of the nursery. The arrangement of the room, the kinds of furnishings, the patterns and motifs all play a part in creating a nursery that relates to the preferences and life-styles of boys. It has been said that boys prefer rooms that resemble workshops or gyms; both the look of the room and the way in which the space can be used serve to give the boy nursery its character.

In a famous experiment conducted by the psychiatrist Erik Erikson in 1963, aimed at studying how children of both genders use play space, 150 boys and girls were individually invited to construct imaginary scenes from a varied collection of blocks, dolls, toy animals, and cars. The researchers' findings have become standard textbook material in developmental psychology. The boys built large, elaborate shapes and left their interior spaces clear. They were excited by construction and motion. They placed their toy animals outside, in the wild. Their energies were outward-going. The tiny baby rocking in his cradle may seem far removed from this kind of almost clichéd boyishness, but according to child development experts, long before his changing table becomes obsolete he will probably sit bolt upright in his stroller and point excitedly at a helicopter, high up in the sky.

◀ *This boy's fascination with cowboys and Indians is reflected in his brightly painted bucking bronco headboard and cowboy dresser (complete with holsters for toy pistols) and hitching post for a hobbyhorse, left. Plaid sheets and Indian weathervane emphasize the theme, while peach-colored walls and delicate window shade provide a light and airy contrast to the room's boyish qualities.*

As Erikson's and subsequent studies have shown, little boys enjoy large-scale things, like big toys. Because they love to build and move, boyish nursery design today tends to favor open space and sturdy, functional, climbable, preferably minimal furnishings — for instance built-in, modular pieces, rugged, country-style furnishings, or chunky, architectural storage units. Boys find construction fun to do, and interesting to look at, making primary-colored, high tech cribs, storage units, and chairs almost as fascinating as scaffolding.

The fascination held by boys for all forms of transportation has long been recognized. In the early nineteenth century, sailing ships, steamboats, and coach scenes enlivened the walls of little boys' nurseries and rocking horses or hobbyhorses stood at the ready. Today, sailing ships have been replaced by cars and trucks on wallpapers and fabrics, and boys rock on everything from dinosaurs and frogs to rabbits or even Babar the Elephant. Collections of toy vehicles, often antique, line open shelving, and a big, round earth or moon globe suggests distant travel.

Animals, generally wild and often extinct, probably represent some of the most popular of boys' nursery motifs. Today, they appear on bedding, drapes, hangings, wallpapers, and in all kinds of painted wall and floor decorations. One company even produces soft, dinosaur-shaped pillows in their range of nursery furnishing fabrics. Animal images, whether cartoonish, childlike, realistic, or simplified, have been incorporated in the most innovative of ways — scenes from Rudyard Kipling's *Jungle Book* painted as murals on the walls of one nursery; elephants marching in a processional frieze, trunk to tail above a picture rail; huge, wooden cutout zoo animals attached to sky-painted walls.

Familiar, favorite animal characters with distinct and childlike personalities, whether it is the three bears or Peter Rabbit, often become a child's best friends. Whether they take the form of hand-painted decoration, stuffed animals, or printed fabrics and papers, these characters can serve as important projections of the child's personality and imagination.

▶ *Colorful car and truck sheets brighten this boy's room decorated in intense primary colors, right. The tubular metal bunk bed and chair give the room a jungle gym effect, with plush carpet waiting to soften any tumbles. A parrot, tiger skin, and glowing Empire State Building reveal the eclectic and idiosyncratic nature of some children's taste in decor — individuality that should be encouraged.*

▶ *This room for an older girl, right, has an old-fashioned garden flavor with its white picket fence radiator cover, white wicker, and floral prints. An old trunk painted white resembles a treasure chest — a perfect place to keep clothes and props for fantasy dress-up.*

▲   *Hearts and flowers, plus a finely crafted bed for a special doll, are enough to give this room, above, the fresh and pretty domestic atmosphere that many little girls enjoy.*

▶   *The same room's hand-painted bunny motif on the headboard is reflected in the bedside rabbit lamp and in a fancifully clothed soft rabbit on the bed, right, both with sleepily floppy ears to invite sweet dreams.*

▲ *Light blue can be a "girl's color" too—in fact, pale blue and pink, and also their primary relatives, bright blue and red, are many girls' favorite combinations. The pale blue upholstered armchair, above, is complemented by the red and blue balloon curtains, and by the red and blue patterned wallpaper border. In both, the delicate, floral prints and white ground help to identify them as feminine in the most traditional sense.*

◀ *A white-painted Chippendale-style bed lends a gracious touch to a young girl's room, left. An eyelet bed skirt and lace-trimmed pillows in fabric matching the delicately sprigged wallpaper unify the room and balance the formality of the bed with a countrylike freshness. A pastel soft sculpture and beribboned hat on the wall are additions specific to the room's occupant.*

SHARED SPACE

"Someone's been sitting in my chair," squeaks Baby Bear, "and has broken it." According to Bettelheim, Baby Bear represents the sibling whose own territorial identity is put at risk by the Goldilocks invasion. When two children, whether of the same or different ages and genders, share a room, every aspect of nursery design comes into play as a means of restoring domestic tranquility.

Once upon a time, two or more children generally shared a room; before the beginning of the nineteenth century, the eldest child was generally favored with the best of everything the nursery had to offer. Today, we know that a measure of equality in the nursery soothes sibling rivalries and that, as Joan Kron writes in *Home-Psych: The Social Psychology of Home and Decoration*, "the more territorial people are, the better they seem to get along."

Yet individual territories within the same room have to be subtly defined, if not for aesthetic, then for psychological reasons. The well-known postmodern architect Robert Venturi once designed a master bedroom for a couple that was divided down the middle, with a different color scheme, a closet with a name on the door, and half the bed on each side. Before long the couple apparently divorced. Instead of the struggle of entirely separate schemes made to coexist within the same room, nursery arrangements and decorating details generally serve to demarcate territories within a space and establish individual, gender, or age specific identities.

A nursery shared by a small girl and her older brother was divided into three areas—a sleeping loft area and personal, underloft storage and play area for each, and a larger, communal play area with table and chairs and shared storage for games. In another nursery, adjacent twin girls' beds were separated from each other by a fantastic play-palace construction.

Folding screens, either of the simple, grid variety thrown over with a length of pretty fabric or a shawl, or playful, shaped, and painted screens designed specifically for children are sometimes used to create a sense of privacy in the

▶ *An older baby and a brand new infant share this nursery, right, decorated in bright, gender neutral colors and friendly animal motifs that appeal to both boys and girls. Assured of individual design identities from the start, each child has his or her own, personal pattern of bedding, though to promote sharing an assortment of toys is stored in a common basket.*

shared nursery. In one nursery, a screen was covered with a nursery-rhyme fabric on one side and a bold geometric on the other, reflecting the separate identities of the baby girl and her older brother who shared the room. The principle of separate storage for separate possessions has been found to greatly reduce quarrels between siblings. Large, freestanding shelving units occasionally serve as dual-purpose room dividers, with storage for one child on one side, and for the other on the flipside.

The use of symbols of ownership and identity has a long and universal tradition. In the Nubian villages of Egypt, families still paint their doors with images representing the household identity—a steamship, for instance, to show that the head of the family works in shipbuilding. In the nursery, individual toy chests are sometimes painted in each child's favorite color, and stenciled with the names or initials of their owners, or with pertinent symbols such as a train on one and a doll on the other. Closet doors, even beds may be identified in the same way.

Bunk beds are classic in the shared nursery and, like so many nursery products, are now being produced in a wide variety of styles, from country spindle styles to rugged Santa Fe, from basic, natural wood contemporary to high tech tubular metal. Many of these are designed to be transformed very simply into single beds. Trundle beds are also coming back into style, and are often used as space-saving solutions in the nursery that is only occasionally shared, by a college-aged sibling or stepsibling, for instance.

Given the importance of sexual identity in childhood, the shared nursery dilemma is often hardest to resolve when the inhabitants are boy and girl, whether they are twins or of different ages. Often a unisex color scheme is chosen based on primaries or hot, bright hues like turquoise or purple, on neutrals such as white or cream, or on softly mixed colors such as aqua, grayed blue, or apricot. As a way of further demarcating territory and helping to establish separate identities, each child's most decorative special possessions may be stored in full view above his or her crib or bed; beribboned hats, strings of colored beads, and party dresses above one, kites, cowboy hats, and antique toy cars or model airplanes above the other.

A bedside table between two sisters' beds, left, is painted in a morning glory pattern to match the headboards. Identical comforters, bedding, and window shades encourage peaceful coexistence between the sisters.

▶ *This castle bunk bed, right, has equally appealing aspects to its upper and lower beds, one providing an excellent view from the turrets, the other a chance to defend the drawbridge and moat. The bed's ice-cream colors and cartoon styling make it suitable for both boy and girl, who can share the underbed storage drawer—a useful place for storing large board games. Multicolored, personalized rockers, each with a child's name painted on the headrail, make favorite seats.*

▶ *When designing a room for more than one child, it's important to consider dividing the space fairly so that each has a window, or equal access to a desirable feature such as a closet or dresser, right. A symmetrical arrangement often proves the most effective; here, striped wallpaper emphasizes that symmetry, and allows the children to designate a central stripe as the boundary between territories.*

THE KINGDOM: 5
ACTIVITY SPACES

▲ *A real Ficus tree, a picket fence holding toys, a trompe l'oeil rabbit hutch, a carrot coat hook, and a streetlamp planter create an inviting activity space, above.*

I was the giant great and still
That sits upon the pillow-hill
And sees before him, dale and plain,
The pleasant land of counterpane.
From Robert Louis Stevenson,
"The Land of Counterpane"

A little over one hundred years have passed since Robert Louis Stevenson established himself as the first poet to write about the world of childhood from the child's viewpoint. Yet, since the publication of Stevenson's *A Child's Garden of Verses* in 1885, no poet has more evocatively captured the many facets of nursery life, nor more tenderly described that "warm and cheerful room," which represented for him an entire world of the imagination.

"I can speak with less authority of gardens than of that other land of counterpane," wrote Stevenson in a letter to a friend. A delicate child prone to attacks of croup, he had spent the greater part of his early years confined to his nursery. The rest of the house, the domain of elders with its "High bare walls" and "great bare floor," was, except for formal interludes with his parents, closed to him, as it would have been to most Victorian children in England. For Stevenson, nursery life was both interior and exterior world—it was the land of counterpane, the land of storybooks, and the Land of Nod; it could be a block city or a foreign land; it was a boat, a port, a hiding place for found treasures, his kingdom.

NEWBORNS AND INFANTS

After the "kingdom of the cradle," writes child psychologist Bruno Bettelheim in *The Uses of Enchantment* (1977), "no child can help wishing for a kingdom of his or her own." During the first sleepy months of babyhood, life is a constant cycle of napping, waking, and feeding. Since activity spaces for games, for coloring, for rough-and-tumble, or for ABCs seem beside the point at this stage, the infant nursery is naturally focused around the cradle and the rocking or nursing chair. Yet from day one, between opening and closing eyes in sleep, the baby is acutely active — looking, touching, listening, learning to focus, to grasp, and to play — even while being relatively immobile.

The importance of stimulating these kinds of infant activity has been understood for some time — the now ubiquitous crib mobile that Alexander Calder unknowingly spawned was probably the first conscious attempt at infant stimulation. In recent years, style decisions in the infant nursery have been increasingly dominated by the constant stream of new theories on what makes babies thrive — whether the nursery is large or small, a separate room, or a corner of the parents' bedroom. The infant's world is relatively tiny; the crib or cradle, the changing table, a commodious chair, and a loving lap serve as bedroom, playroom, living room, dining room, bathroom, and schoolroom. So design elements, like infant activities themselves, tend to be superimposed one on the other.

Recognizing that most newborns feel most secure in the cocooning warmth that they experienced during their intrauterine months, many parents are opting for cradles, bassinets, or even moses baskets rather than cribs. Babies are less likely to feel "lost" in the comfort and security of these smaller beds. One New York architect, Walter Chatham, found a colorful, flower-shaped laundry basket to serve as a bed for his newborn child. Cribs, too, have become cozier, with the new super-fluffy crib quilts and the revival of romantically canopied and four-poster cribs.

Since babies do much more in their beds than just sleep, nursery accessories — including sheets, quilts, pillows, wall hangings, and bumper guards — have become multipurpose items. Some of the most stylish — whether contemporary or traditional — incorporate features to encourage both sleep and developmental play, from romantic, lace-trimmed musical pillows and mechanical wall hangings, to excitingly tactile, soft-sculptured bumper guards, texturally interesting appliqués in satin or plush, and the stimulating contrasts of patchwork quilts. Infant bedding companies are also beginning to produce coordinating, soft crib toys, from cuddly dinosaurs in pretty prints, to musical mobiles and a fluffy puppy that plays music when its body is extended.

▶ *Patterned lamp shades lend a warm glow to this classic, pastel-colored nursery, right. Prints and patterns, from the patchwork quilt to the wallpaper, window fabric, and hand-painted birds and bows, are gently stimulating for a tiny baby, and create a soft, welcoming atmosphere for late night cuddles and feedings.*

▲ *Contrasting black and white is the key to this type of "infant development" bedding, above. A mix of bold, geometrical patterns is thought to stimulate intellectually by appealing to the baby's as yet undeveloped sense of visual perception.*

Nursery lighting has also become multipurpose. Lamps that glow with a soft warm light, printed shades and whimsical figures on the base, are decorative highlights while, at the same time, incorporating night-lights and baby monitors designed to encourage restful sleep for both babies and parents.

One of the most radical developments in infant nursery accessories is the recent spate of black and white products designed in response to new thinking in the field of developmental psychology. Many now believe that small infants, because their visual receptors are undeveloped, can only see bold contrasts in color, and that black and white contrasts are even more stimulating than geometric, primary-colored patterns.

Black and white nursery style is visually captivating, crisply sophisticated; yet designers have managed to avoid a hard-edged look by working with whimsical mixtures of stripes, dots, spots and circles, and checkerboard borders, and softening the effect with eyelet trim and puffy quilting. Bedding, wall hangings, even lamps and crib toys are adorned with black and white animals—panda bears, Holstein cows, piebald horses, and zebras could become the new and most stylish nursery favorites. Even soccer balls and bull's-eyes are entering the world of the newborn.

▲ *A canopied four-posted crib provides a close and comforting environment for a newborn baby, above, from which he can gaze up at a black and white mobile, which features the configurations to which infants seem to be the most responsive, according to several studies of infant perception — including the essential features of a smiling face. As the baby grows, a brightly colored crib gym provides tactile stimulation and opportunities to develop motor skills.*

▲ *This boldly colored nursery wall hanging serves as both an educational toy and a decorative device with true child-appeal, above. Each of the tiny stuffed toys that peek from the tops of the pockets corresponds to the accompanying letter of the alphabet.*

▶ *Tiny, delicate alphabet letters in the cotton fabric of the crib bumper and soft crib toys, right, are more decorative than educational—but the pattern they produce, combined with the many other patterns and shapes in and around the crib, is stimulating for a baby or toddler.*

▼ *The alphabet lends itself perfectly to the traditional processional nursery frieze, below. Here, the tradition is boldly updated through the use of huge, red plastic letters that are stuck directly onto the wall. The size of the letters and their chunky three-dimensionality give them a strong presence that enhances their educational potential. A huge flamingo mobile hung from the ceiling draws attention in the direction of the frieze.*

THE "EVERYTHING" ROOM

After the first six months or so, infant life begins to change, and with it the nursery often undergoes radical transformations. As babies grow and become mobile — sleeping at night more than napping through the day, exploring space, playing with toys, integrating with the wider world — the question of separate spaces for separate activities comes to the fore. Depending on available space, the nursery makes use of, or is divided into, more than one room, for instance a bedroom and a playroom. Or an all-purpose room is created, incorporating areas for sleep, play, living, and learning, as well as for dressing, cleaning and diapering, and receiving small visitors.

The all-purpose nursery may represent the last remaining vestige of the way rooms were used in the "big houses" of pre-seventeenth-century Europe, before concepts of privacy led to the development of bedrooms, living rooms, and so on. It was this kind of room — in which with the help of collapsible beds and tables people would sleep, eat, relax, wash, conduct business, and entertain friends — that spawned the idea of the curtained, four-poster bed. The four-poster crib or twin bed is, for today's busy nursery, a romantic way of enclosing the sleeping area, of separating it from the distracting, daytime world. In some nurseries a bunk bed serves a similar purpose: the top bunk providing a form of cozy enclosure plus, as the child grows, an extra bed for the occasional guest.

> *My bed is like a little boat;*
> *Nurse helps me in when I embark;*
> *She girds me in my sailor's coat*
> *And starts me in the dark.*
> From Robert Louis Stevenson,
> "My Bed Is a Boat"

Stevenson eloquently showed that, given the capacity of children to invent worlds and to imaginatively transform reality into fantasy, furnishings in the all-purpose nursery often serve several activities. Four-poster beds become houses by day, bunk beds turn into castles, pillows may be hills. Though less flexible, fanciful beds shaped as cars, castles, or boats are ready-made for play. Lightweight, scaled-down furnishings that even a toddler can move with ease provide endless possibilities for games, lounging, or napping, and are now produced in a wide range of styles, from country to Victorian. A stylish, foam-filled chaise longue might be a horse for two at playtime, a good place for a nap at naptime, a sickbed for a couple of days, and a perfect prop for an impromptu princess performance. Two scaled-down club chairs with matching ottomans turn into a plane or train and, rearranged, make a place for quiet reading. A child-sized upholstered sofa is a cozy storybook nook that pulls out into a bed for an overnight guest.

▶ *A curtained bed, complete with night-light and bookshelf, creates a cozy "room" within a multipurpose nursery, right. By day, with the curtains tied back, the bed serves as a comfortable and attractive sofalike area from which to sing lullabyes to a sleeping doll. The doll-sized table and chairs can be moved about to accommodate tea parties or playschool for teddy bears, or they can be cleared away to make plenty of space for more active play.*

The use of folding screens has only recently come back into style as a way of flexibly dividing space, and it is a relatively new introduction to the nursery — although the visually rich decoupage or "scrap" screens, which were made by pasting picture-book or magazine images and embossed cake decorations, were popular as draft excluders in Victorian nurseries.

Used to screen off a sleeping area, a changing table, a playspace, or a storage area, folding screens take on a variety of forms from sturdy, child-height, nursery screens cut in fanciful shapes and brightly painted, to simple grid frameworks thrown over with a length of pretty fabric, a special patchwork quilt, or faced with translucent, light-filtering paper. Some nurseries make use of antique scrap screens, or copy the idea in updated fashion. In one child's room, a couple of stretched painters' canvases were hinged together and painted with a leafy country scene. Screens, like so many elements in the all-purpose nursery, are both functional and decorative.

Looking ahead to early childhood, some designers choose to divide the all-purpose nursery horizontally, instead of vertically, by building a loft area over part of the room that can be used as playspace or for sleeping. This has been done even in rooms with average height ceilings; the space beneath the loft area creates a perfect "house" for three-foot-high people. Depending on the style of the nursery, loft areas are supported with anything from rough-hewn timbers, or brightly painted "trees," to Doric columns or supports incorporating shelving.

▶ *A hand-painted "house" screen serves as a fanciful play prop, right. The screen's portability allows for various possibilities in defining activity areas in the child's room.*

The often conflicting requirements of the all-purpose nursery have generated some innovative solutions in nursery style. Any tot knows carpeting to be the perfect cushion for crawling knees and falling bodies, and the ideal surface for lying around on the floor looking at picture books, but any child who has tried pushing a toy car or building a castle on a carpet knows that softness has its limitations. One architect, dealing with the flooring dilemma, cut large squares out of the fitted carpet and filled them with smooth, brightly painted plywood — a yellow, a red, and a blue square.

Because of the need to provide for a variety of activities, style in the all-purpose nursery can become fairly eccentric. But solutions that create multilevels and steps, for instance, or result in obstacles, columns in the center of clear space, chinks, narrow passages, very low spaces, or very dark areas, can be a plus in the nursery. Children enjoy extremes and eccentricities in their physical environment, because they use space physically; secret passageways, tunnels, labyrinths and hiding places have always excited and invited children.

◀ *School-aged children need areas for work and play within their bedrooms, left. An armchair is a cozy place to curl up with a book or a bear, while a built-in desk lit by window light is a good place for letter-writing, doing homework, or just daydreaming. A nautical answer to the rocking horse, the mahogany and pine rocking boat was built in the tradition of wooden boat builders, with an individually numbered brass plate fitted to the hull.*

Perhaps one of the most innovative all-purpose nurseries to have been designed in recent years was created by Windigo, an architectural group comprising architects, designers, craftspeople, engineers, and scientists. Windigo's "fantasy" nursery, exhibited at the group's New York retrospective show, addressed the issue of night and day as they must coexist in any nursery that combines sleep and play. Environment and furnishings—fantastical reinterpretations of fifties style—were designed to be in a state of change. As Windigo describes it: "By the wave of a hand, changes of feeling from sunrise to moonset occurred. Night-lights built into the furniture and sparkling stars built into the ceiling allowed for a soothing, sleep-inducing visual lullaby."

By day, stars turn to sun, night-lights fade, light streams in through the window, and attention turns from the crib with its fin-shaped, rounded, and padded corners, to the playspace that features candy-colored scaled-down seats with lollipop back rests, and a matching triangular stool/trike. During those in-between-play-and-sleep times, a gooseneck floor lamp topped with a teacup-and-saucer shade provides extra illumination. The Windigo nursery, with its fusion of style, technology, and pure fun, could provide a model for the day/night nursery of the future.

▲ *Child-sized dolls or animals such as this pig-lady in her apron and cap, above, make wonderful props for the playroom equipped with small-scale furniture.*

▶ *Neutral carpeting, delicate wallpaper pattern, and basic play furnishings provide a simple, spacious setting for a child's imaginative play, and for the brightly colored artwork and toys of the playroom, right.*

THE PLAYROOM

The great day nursery, best of all,
With pictures pasted on the wall
And leaves upon the blind —
From Robert Louis Stevenson, "To Minnie"

When Robert Louis Stevenson was a small boy, the ideal nursery was in fact two nurseries — the day nursery and the night nursery. Writing in the mid-nineteenth century, health educator William Walcott stressed the importance of two rooms, one of which could be aired while the child played in the other. Today, the ideal nursery still consists of two rooms — a small bedroom and a larger living/playroom. Some babies, such as Beatrice, royal daughter of the Duke and Duchess of York, enjoy the privilege of an entire nursery suite. Nurseries intended specifically for sleeping, living, or playing and learning take on unique qualities determined by the activity for which they are designed.

Small children need to play every day, come sun, snow, or sore throat. And everyday play can range from something as sedentary as piecing together a jigsaw puzzle to something as boisterous as cops and robbers, making both spatial and atmospheric demands on the playroom. The ideal playroom is large, multifaceted, flexible, and inviting — as Selma Fraiberg writes in her book *The Magic Years* (1959), "an island in our world of reality where [the child] can command the creatures of his imagination through play." Many designer-parents believe that the ideal playspace, by remaining relatively neutral and unimposing when it comes to color and decorative elements, serves as a neutral background for the child's toys, paintings, and constructions. Environmental psychologists add that the child can more easily take command over this world of play if the elements within it are scaled to his or her size.

The issue of scale was central to many playrooms designed by architects of the late nineteenth and early twentieth centuries, playrooms that any child today would envy. These rooms, far from being styled according to some notion of a children's aesthetic, were designed to appeal to small people playing at being big people. The most remarkable of these were small playhouses — such as Hans Maria Olbrich's famous Darmstadt cottage for the little Princess of Hesse, who before her death at the age of six would spend entire days there blissfully inventing her own domestic world with child-sized furnishings and dolls. The cottage, entirely scaled to the child, consisted of a parlor and kitchen, simply furnished in Vienna Secession–style yellow pine, with an exquisite grandfather clock, shutters at the windows, and colored glass panels in the front door. Another example is Richard Morris Hunt's play cottage at The Breakers, Rhode Island, with its tiny piano, and its cozy fireside nook under a low arched ceiling. These tiny, whimsical, but completely detailed replicas of cottages were designed to correspond absolutely to the adult world.

Sometimes the contemporary playroom, reinterpreting these playhouses of old, creates a miniature domestic environment that integrates fully with the rest of the house, with the help, perhaps, of a set of child-sized furniture, small cabinets, a Peter Rabbit tea set — all the details that might be found, similarly styled but on a larger scale, in the living room — plus a door knocker.

▶ *Banquette seating covered in garden green makes a quiet, intimate area in this large playroom for two girls, right, and helps to define the raised art area beneath the skylight. An exposed brick wall and trellising echo the playroom's English garden theme.*

▲ Designed to keep a child's toys or hats and mittens out of the way of play, this plastic chain with attached hooks has been used in this nursery, above, as a kind of jungle vine from which stuffed animals hang at the ready.

◄ A child's room is his or her castle in this innovative design, left. Multilevels, narrow passageways, cutout viewing shapes, crawl holes, and a bed up on the ramparts make this room fascinating both for physical activity and pretend play, and for sleep.

Frank Lloyd Wright considered the ideal playroom to be a space suggesting at the same time the shelter of inside and the freedom of outside. This is an idea shared by many. It has been interpreted by designers in a variety of ways, generally incorporating uncluttered and unstructured space, flexible elements, skylights if feasible, a minimum of decoration, and tough, basic materials. In today's play nursery the indoor/outdoor quality may be created with little more than scaled-down Adirondack chairs or even child-sized folding or deck chairs that are stacked away when energy levels are high, vinyl floor tiles in a checkerboard pattern that becomes a built-in games board, and a tubular metal jungle gym, or a ride-on space shuttle. On the other hand, the garden analogy may be stressed to become a theme, with real or faux latticework, green carpeting, earthenware planters, and even a picket fence separating activity areas.

Because they are intrinsically unfussy, bright, and sturdy, updated folk or country styles are often chosen for nursery playspaces — the robust, yet decorative simplicity of what has come to be known as Santa Fe style, for instance, with its organic curves, rounded corners, and colors. In one reinterpreted Southwestern nursery the yellow plank floor, bordered with a hand-painted pattern of green and hot pink lizards, has been left clear except for a small art or snack area defined by handcrafted wooden bench seats with swan-shaped backs, on either side of a long trestle table, and a low, fancifully painted wooden cupboard for toys. Across another corner of the playroom is stretched a multicolored low-slung hammock that serves as a gentle swing, for those moments when it seems like a nice idea to lie back and gaze at the ceiling.

The large, rugged attic room, with its appealing world-of-its-own aura, tends to be the kind of space toward which children gravitate. The architectural complexity of the typical raw attic, with its dormer windows, sloping roof, posts and beams, is especially intriguing, as fascinating to a child as the inner workings of a clock. A few treasure chests filled with toys, a rocking horse (or tyrannosaurus, rabbit, cow, boat), a folk-painted table and chairs set, and the attic becomes an exciting playspace.

One attic room in Texas was transformed into a unique adventure playspace for three young boys by architect Mark Wellen, who replaced some interfering load-bearing walls with rough sawn posts and beams, and lined the space with custom-made wooden blocks and boxes — a series of hollow blocks making giant steps for jumping, climbing, racing cars over, as tables for pasting and coloring, or just for sitting on, and the boxes for hiding in and storing toys. The entire space was painted an unimposing warm gray and white; the toys themselves, and whatever else the children may add, such as paintings or collages, provide the element of color.

The issue of color can be a tricky one in the playroom. Children are not only drawn to color, they seem to attract it like magnets. The newborn infant may have only a few, discreetly colored stuffed animals and a natural wood rattle. But soon the playroom begins to fill with colors — colored toys of every kind; easels with pots of colored paint and huge sheets of paper dripping red, yellow, and blue; fluffy, brightly colored characters; tacky trinkets and mementos; and all the little and big, precious and incidental, accumulated things that a child will want to keep and display, even though they do nothing to enhance the color scheme of the wallpaper.

Schemes that best stand up to this jumble of shades and hues tend to be simple and based on white, cream, or neutral, or those more adventurous light, clear, yet fairly saturated ice-cream colors that are strong enough to back up the hot, bright plastics, yet delicate enough to enhance the natural woods, the subtle fabrics, and the colored stains of carefully designed toys.

▲ *Keeping large, heavy toys like trucks and dollhouses on lower shelves makes them safe and easy for a small person to reach and put away, above. Baskets for storage of assorted smaller toys makes cleanup simple and fast.*

▲ *A dresser with shelves next to the changing table, above, holds an assortment of toys ready to be thrust into the hands of a baby too restless to lie still for a change of clothes or diaper.*

ROOMS FOR LEARNING

Playrooms for small children are by nature also rooms for learning. Ever since 1876 when a man named Milton Bradley published his revolutionary book *Paradise of Childhood*, the educational value of play, and the fun of learning, have been increasingly accepted precepts in the design of both toys and nurseries. And the proliferation in recent years of preschool toys, books, and games designed to teach and amuse simultaneously — from baby flashcards to anatomically correct baby dolls and bright new versions of stacking blocks — has turned many playrooms into virtual schoolrooms.

Robert Louis Stevenson, writing of his day nursery, recalled the pictures pasted on the wall showing "the wars about Sebastopol," as well as plunging ships, bleating sheep, and children from foreign lands. Victorian nurseries were decorated with pictures intended to instruct the child about everything from historical battles to geography; Frank Lloyd Wright's mother, having already decided that her son would be an architect, decorated his nursery walls before he was even born with architectural prints of English cathedrals.

Very often the wallpaper used to decorate the Victorian nursery was instructional, too, whether it was scenic, literary, documentary, or botanical; for the Victorian mother, these wallpapers and pictures were visual aids used in teaching daughters (sons were in school) about the world beyond the nursery. Today's range of nursery wallpapers, hangings, rugs, and so on includes several that, while less overwhelming than the Victorian versions, are printed with ABCs, numerals, maps, scenes from classic fairy tales, planetary configurations, and a number of other subjects that may be absorbed during idle moments or used as a basis for a variety of games.

▶ *Wallpaper with numbers and letters can provide a pleasant diversion for the small child waiting for sleep to come, or waiting for parents to wake in the morning, right.*

In one nursery, a small wall was covered in huge world maps that were pasted to the wall and sealed, adding not only interest, but also seas of blue and many-colored nations to the room. In another, the dado was painted with flat black chalkboard paint, and the picture rail replaced with a "chalk rail" — a length of bright-painted wooden molding suitable for keeping colored chalks. The resulting child-height activity wall, with its ever-changing decoration in chalky blue, pink, yellow, and purple, is a decorative learning tool that welcomes the child's persistent urge to scribble all over the walls.

Children's bedrooms have also become places for learning, as evidenced by the fact that early childhood specialists and preschool toy designers have become involved in the design of educational nursery bedding lines that come complete with attachable props and parents' guides. Educational bedding, say the experts, makes bedtime an interactive learning experience between children and otherwise busy parents. The comforters, sheets, bedspreads, and matching wall hangings are based on topics as diverse as dinosaurs, road safety, and farmyard animals. Other learning products for the night nursery are the glow-in-the-dark mobiles and wall and ceiling decorations, featuring a universe of constellations and planets for young would-be astronomers.

Early childhood literacy has become a major subject of concern for parents today, and it is widely agreed that the best way of encouraging reading is to involve children in literature in their day-to-day lives. The nursery, whether it is a day or night nursery — an obvious channel for literary stimulation — can also become a place imbued with fantasy when scenes or characters from fairy tales are an integral part of its decoration.

Fairy-tale images may be found on nursery bedding or wall coverings, or copied from book pages onto walls and furnishings, or pasted directly onto decoupage nursery screens. In late Victorian days, scenes from fairy tales and nursery rhymes were often found on decorative ceramic nursery tiles that were inlaid into furnishings or hung in panels on walls; later, when nursery tiles went out of style and were no longer manufactured, plain tiles were sometimes hand-painted with fairy-tale themes, or with scenes from classics such as *Aesop's Fables*.

The nursery frieze, which brings into play the idea of sequence as one follows it around the room, is an ideal form for narrative. Many of the most successful Victorian wallpaper friezes were done by children's book illustrators, and since then several have been based on well-known characters from children's literature, such as Pooh Bear, who in one frieze is pictured having just discovered the North Pole, while all around the room little stray figures of Pooh's friends rise up out of the endless frozen landscape. Another favorite story for nursery friezes has been Noah's Ark, with its long procession of diverse animals. However they find their way into nursery decor, scenes from a child's or parent's favorite tale not only introduce the child to literature, but also help that literature to live in the child's imagination long after storytime is over.

◀ *Bulletin boards make a constantly changing gallery of children's artwork, left. With a good work surface directly below, creations can be pinned up for display as soon as they're finished.*

THE NIGHT NURSERY

Last, to the chamber where I lie
My fearful footsteps patter nigh,
And come from out the cold and gloom
Into my warm and cheerful room.
From Robert Louis Stevenson,
"North-west Passage"

Plagued as a little boy by periods of insomnia brought about by illness, Robert Louis Stevenson grew to understand what makes a child's bedroom feel safe and inviting after the lights go out. The great day nursery where he played was "best of all," but it was the atmosphere of his night nursery that he recalled most vividly, and that helped to chase away mean shadows.

Unlike the day nursery, designed to ensure a child's amusement for hours on end and built to survive the ravages of joyful play, the night nursery or bedroom is designed for the demanding task of guiding the child to bed and into the peaceful Land of Nod. The playroom has as its occupant a willing participant in fun; the bedroom is charged with luring that sleepy-eyed but resistant occupant away from play, with promises of a feather-soft, golden-lit, snuggly warm interlude. The night nursery is designed for the transition between waking and dreaming — for bedtime stories, reassuring hugs, a cuddle with a bear — as much as for sleep.

The nursery bedroom often sacrifices spaciousness for the sake of atmosphere — a small, cozy, quiet room that can be taken in at a glance, a room without those dark corners or shadowy recesses that are intriguing by day but menacing at night. The nursery bedroom need not be much larger than the sum of its essential furnishings: a crib, or bed, and side table; a comfortable chair or love seat for cuddles, picture books, and late night feedings; a closet for clothing and bed linens; perhaps drawers; and maybe a changing table. All the other elements added to the nursery bedroom — surface decoration, floor and window coverings, and accessories like bedding, clocks, book-shelves, lamps and night-lights, and pegs — work together with the essentials to convey a mood conducive to tenderness and sweet dreams.

Some nursery bedrooms work by creating a mood through specific themes and fantasies. For, while to create fantasy in the playroom may be seen as imposing on the child's imagination, in the night nursery such focusing of the imagination can make bedtime comfortingly predictable. There are highly romantic little bedrooms, either the romanticism of the ornate Victorian nursery with a sleigh bed, or the more homespun romanticism of a flowery, country cottage nursery with an iron bedstead under the eaves. There are storybook bedrooms: the kind that seems to be taken out of a storybook, with cuckoo clock and cutout hearts; and the kind that is peopled with painted storybook characters and scenes. There are barnyard bedrooms, outer space bedrooms, Disney bedrooms. However such fantasies are created — with murals, stenciled friezes, or pictures on the wall; with printed fabrics, bedding, and wallpapers; with novelty lamps and clocks; or with stuffed animals, dolls, and figurines — they offer the child a wealth of detail, and in many cases a cast of friendly characters, to fill the time before sleep with restful fun, and to wake up with each morning.

▶ *Soft lighting, soft textures, and soft colors in a sketch of a sleeping infant in the night nursery, right, help to create a tranquil atmosphere.*

Color, texture, and light are all powerful conveyors of mood that influence one another. Calming colors that respond well to incandescent light, such as peach and apricot, ivory and buttersquash; mottled effects and washes of warm color; gentle, diffuse lighting without strong shadows; extra-soft or fluffy carpeting and upholstery—these are the qualities most sought after in the child's bedroom. Darker colors are also used. In one bedroom the soft glow of a nursery lamp is reflected in gold-leaf wing shapes that pattern the mottled, blue and black wall.

Ceilings, which tend to be a point of focus in nursery bedrooms, are sometimes painted or papered in deep twilight or sunset shades, thereby perceptually lowering the ceiling and creating a comforting, enclosing vertical space. In their 1913 nursery design for the now famous Omega Workshops showroom in London, Duncan Grant and Vanessa Bell created an entire fantasy with a shelf of large, hand-made wooden animals with moveable limbs, set against painted wall murals whose animals and trees, predating the paper cutouts of Matisse, extended all the way up and over the ceiling—the surface most often looked at by babies lying on their backs.

Many small children accept bedtime as a ritual, and even the smallest deviation—a missing bear, a different blanket, a chair out of place—can upset the routine. Because the bedroom, unlike the playroom, tends to benefit from predictability rather than from flexibility, built-in and all-in-one types of furnishings are often used. Built-in closets and shelves, and beds or cribs that incorporate night tables, changing tables, or drawers, as well as wall sconces and other installed fixtures—these are easy, predictable, and often space saving.

◀ *A quilt hung on the wall by the crib provides a soft, comforting landscape for gazing into as the baby drifts off to sleep, left. Simple pictures composed of delicately printed fabrics give the baby an opportunity to distinguish large shapes or more detailed patterns.*

The bedtime ritual generally ends with the dimming of nursery lamps and the lighting of the night-light. In Victorian days the night-light held a candle; a favorite form was the ceramic cottage that, glowing with candlelight, would be placed on the windowsill to magically keep out the monsters of the dark night. Today, the night-light may be a giant, incandescent crayon, or a plug-in, lit-up unicorn. It may light automatically when the light fades, it may be a glow-in-the-dark fixture, it may incorporate a baby monitor, or it may simply be the bedroom lamp itself, dimmed for sleep. Like every other element in the child's nursery, the night-light has become a significant element of style, influenced by new technologies and shaped by a changing aesthetic. Yet the night-light remains what it always was, a reassuring glow that belongs to the experience of childhood, along with fairy tales and building blocks. When Mrs. Darling, in J. M. Barrie's 1904 classic *Peter Pan*, calls night-lights "the eyes a mother leaves behind her to guard her children," she might very well have been speaking to a young child of the 1990s.

▲ *The essential elements of the baby's night nursery, above, need be little more than a crib and a comfortable chair large enough for bedtime cuddles and stories, and late-night feedings.*

▶ *For an older child the bedside table or chest, right, provides a surface for all the things that help make bedtime comforting — a lamp for reading or quietly looking at picture books, a friendly stuffed animal for company, and a tiny trunk overflowing with treasures. The distinctive sleigh bed adds a touch of fantasy.*

6
NURSERY PRODUCTS

▲ *Matching clothes hampers and other nursery products, above, can lend a finishing touch to the nursery design scheme.*

While the Duke and Duchess of York, Andrew and Fergie, awaited the birth of their first child, newspaper stories on both sides of the Atlantic flapped over Fergie's purchases for the latest royal nursery.

Something new was happening within the Royal Family. The Duchess of York was not content to simply order the very best matching set of nursery furnishings from the very best London department store. Instead, she had been rushing out on discreet, personal shopping sprees, visiting stylish little stores and boutiques around town and picking out a romantic, hand-painted four-poster crib here and a scaled-down, bunny-strewn sofa there. Yet, though her approach to furnishing the royal nursery broke with convention, the press had to admit that Fergie had created an exquisite, fairy-tale world for the little Princess-to-be.

The Duchess of York's well-publicized nursery shopping sprees were indicative not only of changing patterns in royal life-styles, but also of the recent boom in stylishly designed nursery products to suit every kind of home. Until the youngest generation of babies came along, fashion stopped at the nursery door, nursery coordinates were unheard of, and baby products were strictly the realm of a few large companies. But now fashionable baby products, many made by small specialized companies and distributed through specialty stores and catalogs, are flooding the market. And parents, committed to creating rich, stimulating, personalized environments for their children, are sifting through this vast new range of options, piecing together original nurseries with a variety of innovative products from many sources.

Personalizing the nursery has come to mean more than applying a few bunny decals on a standard crib. Furnishings are being custom designed and built; and ready-made furnishings, whether they were bought as sets or individual pieces, are being customized with hand-painted designs, cookie-cutter–shaped cutouts or handholes, and special effect paint treatments. Many of the pieces being bought for today's nursery—whether handcrafted, hand-painted, or exquisitely detailed using the finest materials—are intended to be passed down through generations to come, reviving the custom of the family heirloom.

Yesterday's heirlooms are valued for their decorative qualities, yet many parents today hesitate to put them to use in the nursery because their outmoded design sometimes makes them either impractical or unsafe—as Duchess Fergie pointed out when she turned down the Queen's offer of the silk-lined wrought iron cradle that had rocked royal babies since Queen Victoria. Yet some parents feel that as long as antiques are sturdy, reasonably practical, and conform to safety standards, nothing can beat the unique, time-worn quality that they can bring to the present day nursery.

The best in nursery products today are designed to be attractive, safe, and practical. Current safety standards are intended to protect babies from the kinds of injuries once inflicted by nursery furnishings and toys; yet today, a safe and practical nursery does not imply a clinical, uninteresting setting. Many nursery products today succeed in combining an Old World quality with functional aspects that are strictly modern. Easy-care materials and finishes, space-saving designs, and dual- or even multi-purpose furnishings are becoming commonplace. One product, a true feat of engineering, transforms into fifteen different functions, becoming in turns cradle, high chair, stroller, carriage, rocker, car seat, and more.

An increasing number of furnishings are being designed to be "growable," converting from crib to bed, for instance, or from changing table to desk, as babies quickly grow into toddlers and small children. The Abracadabra Baby Set, by British designer Brian Trianis, converts very simply from crib to play yard, to junior bed, two seats and a table, settee, and finally desk.

▲ *Sturdy antiques, such as the turquoise-painted chest and stool, above, lend a time-worn quality to the nursery.*

BEDDING

The first stirrings of a new tide of style in the nursery were apparently felt when, in 1978, an unemployed car salesman took over a tiny, failing children's bedding company called Red Calliope and gave it—and nursery style in general—a bright new future by introducing the idea of coordinated nursery linens, complete with fashion styling. Since then nursery bedding has become increasingly entwined with fashion, and coordinates might include not only sheets, comforters, pillow shams, and dust ruffles, but also bumper guards, wallpapers, friezes, borders, wall hangings, even mobiles, diaper stackers, and canopy covers. Some manufacturers offer matching fabric by the yard that can be used for drapes, roller blinds, or throw pillows. Just as stylish are the many kinds of educational bedding sets being designed to stimulate learning in infants and small children.

Styles in nursery bedding now tend to evolve almost as quickly as styles in fashion, often using the same kinds of fabrics and design details found on boys' and girls' clothing. But with more and more small companies producing specialized lines, the choice is not limited to any current look. Bedding printed with abstract patterns in postmodern colors, or with bold primary-colored geometrics or spatter designs is available for the more sophisticated contemporary-style nursery, as is a variety of simple oxford stripes, plaids, and dots—many of which are imported from Europe. And there are several styles that have a timeless feel, including country inspired prints in dusty pastels with farmyard motifs; traditional patchwork comforters and pillow covers; crisp, white, Victorian-style bedding with lace edging; and heirloom styles with the most delicate of detailing, such as embroidered trim and scalloped edges. Even classic nursery themes, like bunnies, ducks, and circus and zoo motifs, have become more sophisticated, and many ensembles are based on classic themes from nursery rhymes or children's literature.

Some of the most sophisticated bedding ensembles available for the nursery are derived from current interior

▲ *A traditional patchwork comforter in bright colors is complemented by contemporary crib bumper guards in a successful mix of old and new bedding styles, above.*

▶ *Soft sculptures, crib art, and crib mobiles are designed to coordinate with black and white crib bedding for a unified nursery design scheme, right.*

decorating styles. Some, like a "marbleized" print set with silver ties and cording, or hand-painted sets for instance, emulate interior surface treatments; others, such as English inspired floral chintz ensembles or crib bedding in hand-printed Provençal cottons, echo decorating themes in the rest of the house. At least one company makes one-of-a-kind custom down comforters, covers, ruffles, and other bed accessories for the nursery from customer-supplied fabric, repairs and cleans heirloom quilts, adding new down if necessary, and individualizes bedding with embroidered monograms.

New trends in nursery bedding go beyond style itself, making babies' nights more comfortable, and their days more fun. Some companies now offer one hundred percent cotton bedding, and a few manufacturers have introduced children's sheets with higher thread counts to equal the comfort of adult sheets. Soft, puffy comforters, which have virtually replaced top sheets and blankets in the nursery, are not only snug and easy, but often become decorative pieces in themselves. The snuggest are filled with warm European goose down. Many feature complex appliqués or quilting using fabrics of contrasting textures, such as satin and cotton, that become a tactile experience for sense-orientated infants. Some of these comforters coordinate with equally sense-stimulating, soft-sculptured bumper or head guards.

▲ *Many companies now produce coordinated wall-papers and borders, comforters, bumpers, and sheets, above. Some also offer matching fabric by the yard for upholstering furniture or making window dressings, lamp shades, or soft toys.*

◄ *Many of today's handmade quilts are created using traditional designs, but they incorporate fabrics in contemporary prints, colors, and fiber blends, left. Small quilts are perfect for cribs, while larger ones can be used as wall hangings until a child has grown into a larger bed.*

Learning has become a prominent theme in nursery bedding, both for infants and for toddlers and small children. Infant development designs, based on recent findings of developmental psychologists, are intended to attract and stimulate small babies by offering them prints and appliqués with maximum visual contrast. Infant bedding in limited palettes of black, white, and red or one or two other colors comes with simple animal motifs, and in crisp, stylish abstract patterns, such as dots or stripes, usually softened with lace edging.

Bedding with an educational slant is also being designed for older babies and children. One line, designed by an early education specialist, comes complete with a parents' guide and props, encouraging children to match up, for instance, dinosaur footprints on the bottom sheet with silhouettes on the comforter. Also available are intergalactic ensembles, with stars and constellations that glow faintly in the dark, and alphabetical and numerical sets. Other bedding ensembles, some created by toy designers, turn bed into a play environment, with designs like all-star baseball or football prints on sporty green, or sets that come with attachable stuffed toys.

▲ *It's possible to get quilted bedding in just about any color, depicting any theme. Here, above, the heart-shaped gingham balloons held by the bow-tied bears are echoed in the heart-shaped stitching pattern.*

▶ *The popularity of Raggedy Ann and Raggedy Andy makes a handmade quilt, right, a focus around which to build a bedding scheme — with matching sheets, pillowcases, and, of course, at least one of the dolls themselves.*

◀ *Mother Goose with a detachable gosling makes a delightful quilt for bedding or for hanging on the wall, left.*

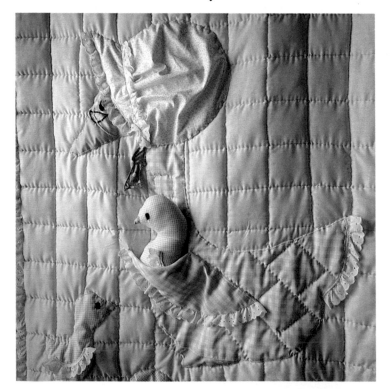

CRADLES AND BASSINETS

One of the many current nursery revivals is the resurgence of the cradle or bassinet as baby's first bed. Criticized for almost fifty years as an unnecessary expense, cradles and bassinets are once again being recognized as ideal sleeping quarters for tiny infants, who feel at their most secure in small, enclosing spaces that ease the transition into the big, wide world. They are easy to move around from room to room, so the baby can enjoy the benefit of daytime company or of a particularly warm and sunny spot. And in those first, often strained weeks after the birth, cradles and bassinets lend a soft, gentle touch to the newly occupied nursery and to parenting.

Many functional alternatives to these tiny beds have been found—from lined and padded drawers, to moses baskets—but the parent who wishes to invest in a cradle or bassinet today has a wealth of options from which to choose. When the time comes to move the baby into a crib, at around four to six months, the bassinet or cradle need not become obsolete. It may serve as a treasured heirloom, or become a pretty and practical storage solution for dolls, stuffed animals, or toys.

Babies have been rocked to sleep in cradles for the past eight hundred years. First developed during medieval times, the cradle began life as a simple chest on rockers, and structurally it changed little until the eighteenth century, when suspended cradles were developed to keep babies off drafty floors and to save mothers' backs from repeated bending and lifting.

Today, both kinds are available in a range of styles. Many come ready-dressed with linings, bedding, and if the construction doesn't include a hood, with gauzy, light-filtering canopies. Some are handcrafted in wood and modeled on the Early American cradle on rockers, with a wooden canopy hood originally intended to keep out drafts. Victorian-style oval-shaped, white-enameled iron cradles, which work on the suspension principle, are also available, as are spindle cradles, and wicker cradles and bassinets. Those with spindle or otherwise open sides have the advantage of allowing the baby to look out at the world, instead of just up at the ceiling.

For those who like cradles but not the frills and ruffles that tend to go with them, European manufacturers are producing some stylish modern and contemporary designs: a British design firm, Tecta, has reproduced Peter Keler's classic Bauhaus cradle; Geuther, a German manufacturer, has designed a minimal, black and white cradle softened with a gauzy canopy. In another departure from tradition, technology has entered cradle design in the form of at least one battery-powered, self-rocking "day" cradle—perhaps inspired by a Victorian cradle taken from a design by Thomas Sheraton, now in London's Victoria and Albert Museum, which had a clockwork movement allowing the cradle to rock nonstop for forty-eight hours.

▶ *This oval, suspended iron cradle, right, is an heirloom that has rocked babies in the family for three generations.*

▶ *An old-fashioned baby carriage is a good daytime bed for napping infants, right. It can be wheeled from room to room, or out into the garden on a sunny day.*

◀ *A sturdy wicker bassinet, hooded and mounted on wheels for moveability, makes a cozy and convenient infant's bed, left.*

▲ *A hooded pink and white wicker cradle with matching chair, and a Victorian-style, white-enameled iron hanging cradle, above, share an heirloom quality that suits the traditionally styled nursery.*

Cribs with two drop sides, one on each side, offer the most versatility when it comes to arranging nursery furniture. European sized cribs are also available. Slightly smaller, and therefore more space-saving than an American crib, the European version generally fits a child up to the age of three — by which time most babies are ready for a bed with or without side rails. Some new cribs offer one-hand, or even no-hands drop side release. Cribs with the widest range of adjustable mattress heights have the longest life. When a baby is finally tall enough to climb out of the crib with the mattress at its lowest level, that crib has become unsafe as the child could fall.

Recent statistical information on the number of babies killed or injured in crib accidents each year has caused so much alarm that manufacturers are now emphasizing the safety factor in the cribs they produce. Nevertheless, sometimes stylish design leads to compromises in safety, and antique or second-generation cribs should be carefully checked for safety features. Parents looking for a sound night's sleep while baby snuggles or bounces in the crib are advised to bear in mind the following guidelines.

Federal safety standards require that there be no more than a 2⅜ inch gap between crib slats. Besides this, cribs with decorative head- or footboards should be checked for openings that might trap or suffocate an exploring child. A snug fit, meaning less than a two-finger gap between the edges of the mattress and the sides of the crib on all sides, is equally crucial. Because toddlers often use cribs for jumping practice, crib construction should be sturdy, with well-secured dowels and knobs, and strong joints. Steel stabilizing bars on each side of the frame give the crib extra stability. Corner posts on cribs lend a classic, storybook look, but the fairy tale can turn sour if the baby's clothing becomes caught. Therefore, experts recommend cribs with corner posts less than ⅝ inch high, or better still no corner posts or decorative corner knobs at all. Teething babies like to gnaw on crib bars and rails, so sharp edges, pinch points around hardware or teething rails, and toxic or chipping paints are potentially hazardous.

▲ *The simplicity of this wooden crib, above, with gracefully arched head- and footboard, makes it fit comfortably into most nursery decors.*

◀ *This oval crib, left, was designed to cocoon a small baby. It has no corners or posts, and no true sides, making it naturally safe and comforting. A glider rocker provides comfort and stability.*

▶ *A child-sized rocker coupled with a scaled-down upholstered chair fit neatly into this tiny nursery, right.*

▼ *The eccentrically shaped, low-seated rattan rocker with a floral print cushion, below, is surprisingly sturdy and will bear up under many years of constant use.*

As the rocking chair developed through time and across the ocean, variations thrived. One of the most comfortable versions, though bulky and often noisy, is the Victorian platform rocker built like an upholstered and sprung arm-chair on gliders. These were intended to eliminate the wear and tear that standard rockers, or "carpet cutters," caused to floor coverings. Combining Early American style with Victorian technique, a Canadian company has come up with a gliding nursery chair and footstool made to resemble a Windsor rocker, with "fan back" fitted cushions in a range of decorator fabrics.

Whatever the style of the rocking chair, it should be of well-designed and solid construction since it is likely to get considerable wear and, in the coming years, some not-so-gentle treatment from children. Those that are simply constructed tend to be the sturdiest. The shape of the runner determines the chair's motion; some rock very gently, others are wild enough to almost tip, though long runners tend to tip less easily. Runners that are narrow and softly pointed, and that do not extend too far forward, help to avoid crushed toes and bruised shinbones. And of vital importance in the nursery is a chair that rocks quietly without squeaks or creaks.

▲ *This contemporary update of the Windsor rocker, above, with extra-wide seat and curved back for more comfortable nursing, was designed especially for the nursery.*

◀ *This scaled-down, handcrafted wicker rocker, left, was reproduced from a vintage 1940s design.*

SCALED-DOWN SEATING

Scaled-down chairs of all descriptions were made for children from the beginning of the nineteenth century. Newspaper advertisements tell of Hitchcock and Windsor chairs, as well as rockers, ladder-back armchairs, settees, and benches of every description. Often, scaled-down chairs were simply adult chairs with sawn-off legs, resulting in squat, incongruous looking pieces with seats that were too deep and arms that were too widely spaced for little bodies. However, the finest examples were in every dimension miniature versions of grown-up models. One of the most successful models for miniaturization was the ubiquitous Windsor chair, which because of its inherent lightness retains its elegance however small it gets. The simple slat-back chair also scales down well and retains its strength easily. This was the model that both the Shakers and William Morris adapted for children.

Today the tradition of scaled-down nursery seating has been revived with some of the most up-to-date styles, as well as several period pieces reinterpreted and scaled for small children. According to environmental psychologists, these scaled-down models help children develop a sense of control over their own small worlds. And since children generally delight in mimicking adult life, meaning the life they see in their own home, seating that reflects the style of furnishing found in the rest of the house can be especially delightful for the nursery.

Scaled-down seats, like the ones found in the living room, kitchen, office, and garden, are about one-third the size of adult versions with seats and arms scaled comfortably for a child, and range from those intended for pure lounging comfort to those that are meant to function in a working environment. Since they may end up doubling as props for playing train, scaled-down seats work best when they are sturdy enough to endure being climbed over, and light enough for small people to move around by themselves. Scaled-down seating should also be well balanced to prevent tipping, and covered in easy-care, preferably stainproof fabrics.

▲ *This miniature classic rocking chair and footstool, above, have been adorned with a custom-painted pinwheel motif to match other furnishings in the room.*

▶ *Designed to be playful, practical, and comfortable, these scaled-down, vinyl-upholstered chairs combine child-like humor with sophisticated wit and style, right.*

The most c
foam construc
seats, some c
child-sized vc
elegant parlo
lounging an
matching pil
Equally hum
big, soft, cozy
out into a be
Other ava
tique—inclu
reinterpretec
classic meta
fect workin,
child-sized
and stool a
design. Ani
classic cha
Willows, of
bear-shape
chairs, inc
Scaled-c
sidered cr
schoolers,
sets, this
table and
turers pro
neat singl
fanciful i
Some cor
crayons a
ufacturer
three dif
chairs sh
a lot of 1
upon to
wide en
may be

▲ *The formality of this elegant, child-sized version of a classic chair is offset by a storybook seat, above, which features a needlepoint based on an illustration from Beatrix Potter's much loved tale The Tailor of Gloucester. The letters of the alphabet framing the picture are an added element of interest.*

◀ *These jazzy, folk art characters, left, sturdily handcrafted and brightly hand-painted with whimsical patterns for today's active children, double as toys and child-sized furnishings in a colorful room.*

◀ *A more elaborate, wicker armchair scaled to child's size, left, is intended for quiet comfort.*

▼ *This primary-colored, foldaway child's chair couples the practicality of plastic and washable canvas with the movability of a simple, lightweight construction that makes rearranging the room easy for even a small child, below.*

ARCHITECTS AND DESIGNERS

ANDERSON-SCHWARTZ
Fred Schwartz
40 Hudson Street, New York, NY 10013
(212) 608-0185
Architecture and design

COURLAND DESIGN, INC.
Mercedes Courland
40 Park Way, Sea Cliff, NY 11579
(516) 759-4802
Interior design and decorative painting

GARY CRAIN ASSOC., INC.
234 East 58th Street, New York, NY 10022
(212) 223-2050
Interior design

ICKEN ASSOC., INC.
Construction and Design Contractors
111 Sandy Hollow Road, Northport, NY 11768
(516) 757-7743

NOEL JEFFREY
215 East 58th Street, New York, NY 10022
(212) 935-7775
Architecture and design

JUST FOR KIDS
Beverly Schnauz
507 Summit, Ridgewood, NJ 07450
(201) 445-6737
Children's room specialist

ALLEN KAUFMAN DESIGN, INC.
150 Fifth Avenue, New York, NY 10003
(212) 675-9045
Architecture and design

TIMOTHY MACDONALD
515 Madison Avenue, New York, NY 10022
(212) 593-4333
Interior design

GINNY MAGHER INTERIORS
2300 Peachtree Road, B-207, Atlanta, GA 30309
(404) 351-4760
Interior design

PAM MARGONELLI
66 Thomas Street, New York, NY 10013
(212) 233-0559
Interior design

MCMILLEN, INC.
155 East 56th Street, New York, NY 10022
(212) 753-5600
Interior decoration

MODEWORKS
37-04 Van Nostrand Place, Douglaston, NY 11363
(516) 759-4802
Interior design and wall graphics

J. P. MOLYNEUX
29 East 69th Street, New York, NY 10021
(212) 628-0097
Interior design

CHARLOTTE MOSS AND CO., LTD.
131 East 70th Street, New York, NY 10021
(212) 772-3320
Interior design and antiques

LUIS ORTEGA DESIGN STUDIO
8813 Rangely Avenue, Suite 3, Los Angeles, CA 90048
(213) 273-2040

FRANK K. PENNINO AND ASSOC.
8654 Holloway Plaza Drive, Los Angeles, CA 90069
(213) 657-8847
Architecture and design

MARTHA STACK, LTD.
353 East 72nd Street, New York, NY 10021
(212) 628-5370
Interior design

VAL ARNOLD AND ASSOC.
221 North Robertson Boulevard, Suite B
Beverly Hills, CA 90211
(213) 276-2215
Architecture and design

STEVEN MARC WASSERMAN ALLIED ASID
Diane Maggid Borenstein
53 East Main Street, Oyster Bay, NY 11771
(516) 922-2886
Interior design

WINDIGO
999 Mt. Kemble Avenue, Morristown, NJ 07960
(201) 766-7680
Architecture and design

C. M. WRIGHT
700 North La Cienega Boulevard, Los Angeles, CA 90069
(213) 657-7655
Interior design

DECORATIVE PAINTERS/MURALISTS

CARYL HALL STUDIOS
143 Main Street, Cold Spring Harbor, NY 11724
(516) 367-8777

BAGON RYLEZ
209 Seventh Avenue, Brooklyn, NY 11215
(718) 788-9192

JAMES ALAN SMITH
153 East 88th Street, New York, NY 10128
(212) 876-4660

SUITE DREAMS
Kathleen Spicer
640 Broadway #3, New York, NY 10012
(212) 533-6467

MICHAEL THORNTON-SMITH
123 Chambers Street, New York, NY 10007
(212) 619-5338

TROMPLOY, INC.
400 Lafayette Street, New York, NY 10003
(212) 420-1639

MANUFACTURERS AND IMPORTERS

AMISCO INDUSTRIES, LTD.
33 Fifth Street, L'Ilset, Quebec, CAN, GOR 2CO
(418) 247-5025
Colorful, tubular metal beds, bunks, furnishings, and accessories.

APPALACHIAN HOUSE
1010 Boston Post Road, Darien, CT 06820
(203) 655-7885
Handcrafted accessories.

BADGER BASKET CO.
616 North Court, Palatine, IL 60067
(312) 991-3800
Wicker bassinets, hampers, cradles.

BELLINI JUVENILE DESIGNER FURNITURE CORP.
1302 Second Avenue, New York, NY 10021
(212) 517-9233
Nursery furnishings and accessories imported from Italy.

BENICIA FOUNDRY AND IRONWORKS, INC.
720 East H Street, Benicia, CA 94510
(707) 745-4645
Cradles, cribs, dressing tables, daybeds, and beds.

BIELECKY BROTHERS, INC.
306 East 61st Street, New York, NY 10021
(212) 753-2355
Scaled-down wicker furniture reproduced from traditional designs. To order.

CHILD CRAFT
P.O. Box 444, East Market Street
Salem, IN 47167
(812) 883-3111
Convertible cribs; coordinating nursery furnishings and accessories in a range of styles.

DUTALIER, INC.
298 Chaput Street, St.-Pie, Quebec, CAN, JOH 1WO
(514) 772-2403
Glider rockers.

E.A.T. GIFTS
1062 Madison Avenue, New York, NY 10028
(212) 861-2544
Including scaled-down furnishings.

FOAM ETC.
P.O. Box 110545, Arlington, TX 76007
(817) 640-6112
Scaled-down period pieces in foam. Will cover in your fabric.

FUN FURNITURE
8451 Beverly Boulevard, Los Angeles, CA 90048
(213) 655-2711
Postmodern, fantasy storage pieces.

KIDS CORP. INTL.
12020 SW 114 Place, Miami, FLA 33176
(305) 255-0014
Importers of contemporary-styled European nursery furnishings and rocking horses.

A. LOCK AND CO.
Williamsport, PA 17705
1-800-233-8467
Rocking chairs.

LEWIS OF LONDON
25 Power Drive, Hauppauge, NY 11788
(516) 582-8300

515 Columbus Avenue, New York, NY 10024
(212) 787-9490
Imported nursery furnishings and accessories.

MARSHALL BABY CARE PRODUCTS
600 Barclay Boulevard, Lincolnshire, IL 60069
1-800-323-1482
Imports nursery furnishings and accessories from Europe, including European-sized cribs and bedding.

NEWBORNE COMPANY, INC.
River Road, Worthington, MA 01098
1-800-237-1712
Nursery furnishings, including self-rocking crib.

TRACERS FURNITURE, INC.
612 Waverly Avenue, Mamaroneck, NY 10543
(914) 381-5777
Contemporary furniture styles imported from Italy.

WICKER GARDEN
1318 Madison Avenue, New York, NY 10128
(212) 410-7000
Victorian-style furnishings and accessories.

SCANDINAVIAN DESIGN
127 East 59th Street, New York, NY 10022
(212) 755-6078
Furniture by Muurame, including Alvar Aalto designs.

SHAKER WORKSHOPS
Box 1028, Concord, MA 01742
(617) 646-8985
Shaker rocking chairs, pegs, baskets, miniatures.

SHERWOOD
P.O. Box 519, Spring City, TN 37381
"Kid's Collection" of child-sized foam flip sofas and chairs.

SIMMONS JUVENILE PRODUCTS CO., INC.
613 East Beacon Avenue, New London, WI 54961
(414) 982-2140
Traditionally styled nursery furnishings, including convertible sleigh crib.

SJL PRODUCTS, INC.
6130 East Slauson, Commerce, CA 90040
(213) 721-4333
Scaled-down foam furniture.

T. C. TIMBER
Habermaass Corp.
Box 42, Jordan Road, Skaneateles, NY 13152
(315) 685-6660
Bauhaus-style play/work furniture in primary painted wood, plus wooden activity toys imported from Germany.

SOFT GOODS AND ACCESSORIES

CALICO COTTAGE, INC.
12974 SW 132nd Avenue, Miami, FL 33186
(305) 233-1404

CALIFORNIA KIDS
525 Fifth Street, San Francisco, CA 94107
(415) 974-5437
Contemporary styled bedding and bed accessories.

CENTURY RUG CORP.
44 West 28th Street, New York, NY 10001
1-800-338-7847
Nursery dhurrie rugs.

THE COMPANY STORE
500 Company Store Road, La Crosse, WI 54601-4477
1-800-356-9367
Machine-washable, European down crib comforters. Plus monogramming service.

COTHRAN AND CO., INC.
P.O. Box 912, Selma, AL 36702
1-800-253-1785

DAN RIVER, INC.
111 West 40th Street, New York, NY 10018
(212) 554-5555
The "Learning Line."

DAYTON'S
700 Nicollet Mall, Minneapolis, MN 55402
(612) 375-2200
Stores throughout Midwest. Bedding and accessories.

DIPLOMAT JUVENILE CORP.
118 Railroad Avenue, W. Haverstraw, NY 10993
1-800-247-9063
Bedding, draperies, etc., including racing car bedding and daybed bedding.

FINE ART PILLOWS AND SPECIALTIES CORP.
601 West 26th Street, New York, NY 10001
(212) 929-0229
French-inspired bassinet bedding and accessories.

GEAR KIDS
127 Seventh Avenue, New York, NY 10011
(212) 645-8000

GLENNA JEAN MANUFACTURING CO.
230 North Sycamore Street, P.O. Box 2187
Petersburg, VA 23803
1-800-446-6018

HEIRLOOM LINENS
1925 West Lake Drive, Burlington, NC 27215
(919) 222-9974
Classic "heirloom" crib quilts.

HOWARD KAPLAN'S FRENCH COUNTRY STORE
35 East 10th Street, New York, NY 10003
(212) 529-1200
French country bedding, fabrics, and accessories.

IMPORT SPECIALISTS, INC.
82 Wall Street, New York, NY 10005
Handwoven, hand-stenciled cotton dhurrie rugs.

LAURA ASHLEY MOTHER AND CHILD STORES
1-800-223-6917

LITTLE VIKINGS
252 Norman Avenue, Brooklyn, NY 11222
(718) 389-0966

MACY'S
151 West 34th Street, New York, NY 10001
(212) 695-4400

180 Peachtree Street NW, Atlanta, Ga 30303
(404) 221-7221

Stockton and O'Farrell, Union Square
San Francisco, CA 94102
(415) 397-3333
Bedding and accessories. Stores above are division headquarters.

MARIMEKKO
112 West 34th Street, New York, NY 10001
(212) 244-7560
Contemporary, Scandinavian-style bedding and coordinating papers.

MOTIF DESIGNS
20 Jones Street, New Rochelle, NY 10801
(914) 633-1170

NOEL JOANNA, INC.
One Mason, Irvine, CA 92718
1-800-854-8760

PIERRE DEUX FABRICS
870 Madison Avenue, New York, NY 10021
(212) 570-9343
Fabrics, bedding, and coordinates in imported Provençal prints.

PRETENDABLES, INC.
402 Coloma Street, Sausalito, CA 94965
1-800-367-5223
Infant bedding with hand-painted embellishment.

RED CALLIOPE AND ASSOC., INC.
13003 South Figueroa Street, Los Angeles, CA 90061
1-800-421-0526

TRINA FOR INFANTS
P.O. Box 1431, Fall River, MA 02722
1-800-558-BABY

WAVERLY
79 Madison Avenue, New York, NY 10010
(212) 213-8100
"Just for Fun" wallpaper collection; colorable wallpapers.

ROOM ACCESSORIES, HARDWARE, TOYS

P.A. BERGNER
331 West Wisconsin Avenue, Milwaukee, WI 53203
(414) 347-5109
Toys and room accessories.

DAYTON'S
Toys and room accessories. See under SOFT GOODS.

EUROPEAN TOY COLLECTION
97 Hillcrest Road, Box 203, Ogden Dunes, IN 46368
(219) 763-3234
Clocks, clothing racks, mobiles, and toys.

GEAR KIDS
Lamps and other room accessories. See under SOFT GOODS.

GLOUCESTER CLASSICS, LTD.
811 Boylston Street, Boston, MA 02116
(617) 424-0027
Handcrafted large-scale toys, including rocking boat with custom-stenciled name.

HELLER DESIGNS, INC.
41 Madison Avenue, New York, NY 10010
(212) 685-4200
Brightly colored or patterned replacement knobs for drawers and closets.

MACY'S
Toys. See under SOFT GOODS.

MILLS RIVER INDUSTRIES, INC.
713 Old Orchard Road, Hendersonville, NC 28739
1-800-627-1089
Country, Victorian, and Southwest style rugs, baskets, child- and doll-size furniture.

MR. MOPPS
1405 Martin Luther King, Jr., Boulevard
Berkeley, CA 94709
(415) 525-9633
Old-fashioned picture blocks.

PAPA JAKES WOODSHOP
P.O. Box 809, Sedalia, MO 65301
(816) 826-7750
Rustic-style work/play set, toys, quilt stand, kindling box.

THE PLAYMILL
R.F.D. # Box 89, Dover-Foxcoft, ME 04426
(207) 564-8122
Personalized animal coat stands and other accessories, to order.

THINK BIG
390 West Broadway, New York, NY 10012
(212) 925-7300
Giant crayon night-lights, oversized blocks, etc.

TOT, INC.
P.O. Box 32239, Washington, DC 20007
(202) 337-1177
Black and white infant development toys and cradle art.

URSA MAJOR
P.O. Box 3368, Ashland, OR 97520
1-800-999-3433
Eight- or twelve-foot, glow-in-the-dark winter or summer sky stencil.

WIMMER-FERGUSON CHILD PRODUCTS
P.O. Box 10427, 13130 South Washington Street
Denver, CO 80210
(303) 733-0848
Infant development crib art and toys.

CUSTOM, HANDCRAFTED OR HAND-PAINTED FURNISHINGS

BASKETS BY ROSELLE
137 Kings Highway, Hauppauge, NY 11788
(516) 234-8873
Hand-painted wicker baskets, rockers, dolls' carriages, etc.

BOSTON AND WINTHROP
2 East 93rd Street, New York, NY 10128
(212) 410-6388

35 Banks Terrace, Swampscott, MA 01907
(617) 593-8248
*Full range of hand-painted nursery furnishings, set patterns
or custom.*

BRIGHT IDEAS
12442 SW 117 Court, Miami, FLA 33186
1-800-842-7555
*Hand silkscreened and painted country-style seating and
coordinating accessories. Plus fun-shaped drawer pulls.*

GALAXY CUSTOM RUG PROGRAM
GALAXY CARPET MILLS, INC.
850 Arthur Avenue, Elk Grove Village, IL 60007
Will produce area rugs to individual specification.

LAURA D'S FOLK-ART FURNITURE
106 Gleneida Avenue, Carmel, NY 10512
(914) 228-1440
Whimsical, handcrafted and painted nursery furnishings.

LITTLE ONE'S HAND PAINTED FURNITURE
P.O. Box 707, Lowe Street, Buchanan, VA 24066
(703) 254-1780
Full range of hand-painted furnishings in set patterns.

PIECES OF DREAMS
2715-J Broadbent Parkway, Albuquerque, NM 87107
1-800-336-6969
Fun, shaped furnishings including work/play sets.

PIPPEN HILL
Box 1031, Rome, GA 30161
(404) 235-3846
Handcrafted furniture and accessories.

BEVERLY SCHMIDT
41 Highfield Road, Glen Cove, NY 11542
(516) 676-2153
*Handcarved and painted three-dimensional trompe l'oeil
figures. By appointment only.*

TAD TAYLOR'S FANTASY FURNITURE
91 Lake Avenue, Greenwich, CT 06830
(203) 629-3990
*Custom-made items include swan rockers, castle bunk beds,
race-car beds.*

ZION'S COOPERATIVE MERCANTILE INSTITUTION
2200 South, 900 West, Salt Lake City, UT 84137
(801) 321-6000
Brass and iron cribs.

MAIL ORDER

BILL BRAGDON
Box 6, Star Route, New Hope, PA 18938
(215) 862-9313
Handcrafted character chairs including cowboy, princess, elephant, or custom order. Designs incorporate bookshelf or toy chest.

BOSTON AND WINTHROP
See under CUSTOM.

CHILDCRAFT
20 Kilmer Road, Edison, NJ 08818
1-800-367-3255
Toy catalog also features furnishings and educational bedding and decorations.

THE COMPANY STORE
See under SOFT GOODS.

CONRAN'S MAIL ORDER
475 Oberlin Avenue South, CN 2103,
Lakewood, NJ 08701-1053
(201) 905-8800

E.A.T. GIFTS
Shipping available. See under NURSERY FURNISHINGS.

FIRST CLASS MAIL ORDER CATALOG
3305 Macomb Street, NW, Washington, DC 20008
(202) 363-3449
Includes unusual scaled-down furnishings.

FOAM ETC.
Drop ship UPS orders available. See under NURSERY FURNISHINGS.

JUST FOR KIDS!
324 Raritan Avenue, Highland Park, NJ 08904
1-800-654-6963
Children's catalog includes some fun furnishings and storage.

LAURA ASHLEY BY POST
1300 MacArthur Boulevard, Mahwah, NJ 07430
1-800-367-2000

MERTZ SPACE EDUCATION CO.
P.O. Box 255, Mansfield, OH 44901
(419) 525-1252
Cosmictudes Planetarium Kit.

MOTHERCARE UK, LTD.
(Catalog request)
P.O. Box 138, Northampton NN3 1WB, United Kingdom
Contemporary, European flavor coordinated bedding, papers, curtains, and accessories.

PENNY WHISTLE
1283 Madison Avenue, New York, NY 10123
(212) 369-3868
Includes some furnishings and large scale toys.

SQUIGGLES AND DOTS
1-800-937-KIDS
Stylish, handcrafted furniture and accessories, including country and Santa Fe styles.

URSA MAJOR
See under ROOM ACCESSORIES.

WEE CHAIRS
P.O. Box 22806, Lexington, KY 40522
(606) 268-1555
Scaled-down upholstered seating.

THE DANNY FOUNDATION
(800) 83-DANNY
Free brochure on crib safety, for new, used, and antique cribs.

PHOTOGRAPH CREDITS

ALL PHOTOGRAPHS BY ANDREW BORDWIN EXCEPT AS INDICATED BELOW

TONY GIAMMARINO: *19, 29, 30, 31 (2), 84, 85, 89 (lower left and right), 132, 135, 166 (left), 179, 188, 198, 200, 202 (2), 252*

STEVE MOORE: *11, 37 (right), 51, 53 (right), 60, 67, 81, 105, 166 (right), 167, 205, 217 (lower left), 219, 220 (upper right)*

MICHAEL THORNTON-SMITH: *230*

© MARK DARLEY/ESTO FOR WINDIGO: *110, 225 (lower left), 231*

DESIGN CREDITS

APPALACHIAN HOUSE: *19, 29, 30, 31(2), 89(lower right), 132, 200, 202(2), 203*

LAURA ASHLEY: *37, 105, 167, 217(lower left), 220(upper right)*

BIELECKY BROTHERS, INC.: *206 (right), 220 (lower left and right), 225 (top left), 229 (2)*

BOSTON AND WINTHROP: *75, 90, 101, 103 (left), 224*

COURLAND DESIGN, INC.: *38, 40, 69, 136, 145, 194, 234*

GARY CRAIN ASSOC., INC.: *11, 51, 219*

FUN FURNITURE: *54*

CARYL HALL STUDIOS: *99, 109, 209, 241*

ICKEN ASSOC., INC.: *102, 121, 122, 160*

NOEL JEFFREY: *70, 118, 124, 125*

JUST FOR KIDS: *23, 28, 88, 131, 150, 182, 201, 206 (left)*

ALLEN KAUFMAN DESIGN, INC.: *13, 36, 79, 80, 110, 223*

LAURA D'S FOLK-ART FURNITURE: *8, 26, 98, 113, 140, 160, 226, 228*

LEWIS OF LONDON: *83, 164, 199, 207, 210*

LITTLE ONE'S HAND PAINTED FURNITURE: *20, 89 (top left), 96, 148, 149, 151, 154, 157, 163, 170–171, 215, 227, 235 (right)*

TIMOTHY MACDONALD: *22, 74*

MCMILLEN, INC.: *41, 169, 172, 174, 175, 244*

CHARLOTTE MOSS AND CO., LTD.: *32, 42, 45, 47, 48, 49, 50, 114, 177*

MOTIF DESIGNS: *16, 27, 34, 35, 37 (left), 146–147, 180, 197, 212, 218, 238*

BEVERLY SCHMIDT: *62–63*

FRED SCHWARTZ: *53 (right), 60, 67, 81, 166*

JAMES ALAN SMITH (MURALIST): *11, 42, 44, 49, 50, 51, 114, 177, 219*

MARTHA STACK, LTD.: *24, 25, 222*

TAD TAYLOR'S FANTASY FURNITURE: *64, 72, 87, 106, 117, 156, 235 (left)*

MICHAEL THORNTON-SMITH: *33, 76, 230*

STEVEN MARC WASSERMAN: *55, 58, 61, 62–63*

WINDIGO: *53 (left), 110, 178, 225 (lower left), 231*

INDEX